The Making of

Lemonade

By Ty Sagalow

outskirts
press

Outskirts Press, Inc.
http://www.outskirtspress.com

Paperback ISBN: 978-1-9772-0798-2
Hardback ISBN: 978-1-9772-0807-1

Dedication

To the employees of Lemonade, the true heroes of this story.

Table of Contents

Story 1: An Ordinary Day 1

Story 2: Meeting Daniel 6

Story 3: Jerusalem 11

Story 4: Who Are We? (and Will Anyone Care?):
The Lemonade Business Model 17

Story 5: $13 Million and Six People 25

Story 6: Building the Team 33

Story 7: Finding a Reinsurer 58

Story 8: Finding a Rating Agency .63

Story 9: Getting Our First License 66

Story 10: The Launch 73

Story 11: Who Are Those Guys? 77

Story 12: Sea to Shining Sea 83

Story 13: A Dream Tested 91

Story 14: One Year Later—Lemonade and Beyond 94

Acknowledgments

This book could not have been done without a collaboration of efforts by many people. The Story of Lemonade is the story of the many people named in the pages of this book, including of course, the founders, Daniel Schreiber and Shai Wininger. In this Acknowledgments page, I will not repeat those names but rather give thanks to the unnamed people who made this book possible.

First and foremost, I would like to thank business historian Alexandra Reed Lajoux, who encouraged me to write this book in my own words, and who facilitated this process as my first reader as the book unfolded. Every Monday night, Alex would graciously listen to me as I gave a story about Lemonade's first two years. She would then compose the chapter story over the week and we would go back and forth editing the chapter until we were both satisfied. More than any other single individual, there would be no Story of Lemonade without Alex. I will forever be in her debt.

I also wish to thank Kelli Christianson of Bibuli, who gave my first full manuscript a thorough professional edit – twice! Also noteworthy were the good people at Outskirts Press, my publisher, especially

Deni Sinteral-Scott who managed the publisher process with care and expertise.

Deep thanks are also due to my cover artist, Chris Smith of QuarterNative.com. I can't say enough about Chris's artistic genius in creating the cover illustration of a lemonade tree with its roots in Israel springing into growth and life in New York City, certainly a picture worth more than the proverbial thousand words.

Finally, I acknowledge my wonderful wife Jane, indeed my "better half", who cheerfully gave up our Monday nights (and sometimes other evenings) during the year it took me to write this account of the "little" company that changed the insurance industry - and my life - for the good.

Ty Sagalow
April 2019

PREFACE:

Redeeming Insurance

Insurance: "A *business that involves selling people promises to pay later that are never fulfilled.*"

That's how the Urban Dictionary, a crowdsourced online source known for irreverence, defines the insurance industry.

Let's face it: Insurance is one of the most hated industries in history. It's up there with dentistry and mortuary services. Why? Because the very model of modern insurance has an inherent conflict between the insurance carrier and its customer. Simply put, the more insurers deny or delay paying claims, the more money they make. It's a one-to-one ratio. Every dollar in a claim denied for the customer is a dollar made for the carrier. This concept was never so well expressed as it was by fourteenth-century merchant Francesco Datini, who complained in a letter to his wife, Margherita, that he was having problems with his insurance company. "For when they insure," he wrote, "it is sweet to them to take the monies; but when disaster comes, it is otherwise and each man draws his rump back, and strives not to pay."

The Way It Used to Be

Once upon a time, insurance was all about helping one another. There was no insurance industry *per se*, at least not like we know it today. Rather, there was an evolution from benign lenders and leaders to communal self-insurance. In *Against the Gods: The Remarkable Story of Risk* (Wiley, 1998), Peter Bernstein traced formal risk transfer back to ancient Babylon (today's Iraq), in the Code of Hammurabi nearly four thousand years ago. Merchants could take out a loan for a voyage, but if their ship sank, they owed nothing. Similar clemency was shown by Roman Emperor Claudius (10 BCE–54 ACE), who used his own funds (presumably sourced from tax revenues) to cover storm losses incurred by merchants in his realm, an early example of the ultimate in governmental insurance program (like today's flood insurance) but for no premium.

As commercial activity began to flourish in Europe, insurance sprang up from communal roots. Farmers formed cooperatives to insure one another. Members of occupational guilds pooled funds to insure one another. Merchants who traveled to the Colonies in America also worked together. In the seventeenth century, this communal form of insurance found distinct expression in coffeehouses all over London, as Markman Ellis recounts in *The Coffee House: A Cultural History*.

All over London, merchants would gather to share risk. Physicians gathered at Child's Coffee House in St Paul's Churchyard, security dealers huddled at Jonathan's, metal dealers congregated at the Jerusalem coffee house, and shipowners and merchants hung out at Garraway's and at a port tavern in London owned by Edward Lloyd (c. 1688–1726). Edward Lloyd's tavern was known for its underwriting, which happened when merchants would all agree to pool their risk and sign on the dotted line to confirm the arrangement while others would simply gamble on the outcome of the voyage.

In this way, merhants would gather at Edward Lloyds, and those who were willing to take on a portion of the risk for voyages would list the amount of the voyage they were willing to insure and sign their names underneath a contract that detailed the terms of the risk. Incidentally, this is how the term "underwriter" came into being.

These activities became so popular that the tavern moved away from the River Thames and moved to Tower Street, becoming, for lack of a better name, a coffee house where each table had paper to write down the risks to be taken and the risk takers who took them. Today (with some nontrivial alterations), we know that original coffee house as Lloyd's of London.[1]

MODERN INSURANCE THEN RUINS EVERYTHING

When institutions arose to take on insurance without embracing this original concept of community, the disappointments soon began. Once there was a financial incentive by a centralized organization separated from its policyholders to deny a claim, the denials seemingly began. Once policyholders felt that their insurance carriers might deny valid claims, they began to fudge on their claim submissions in an attempt to "even things up" (what the modern insurance industry calls "Insurance Fraud"—notice that the term is used to go only one way). And so it was that modern insurance lost the spirit of "we" to become "us vs. them." Insurers believe their customers are liars. Customers assume insurers are cheaters. And it's difficult not to think that way, because the incentives point in that direction.

No one understands the drivers of lying and cheating better than behavioral economist and future Lemonade Chief Behavioral Officer Dan Ariely. The James B. Duke Professor of Psychology & Behavioral Economics at Duke University, Ariely is author of *The Honest Truth About Dishonesty: How We Lie to Everyone—Especially Ourselves* (Harper,

---

1   For a detailed explanation of link between Edwards Lloyds and the rise of Lloyd's of London after his death, see https:apebh2012.files.wordpress.com/2011/05.boyce-commerical-infrastructure-_3_.pdf

2013). He traces dishonesty to its root cause: conflict of interest, which happens to be the subject of his speech called "Beware of Conflicts of Interest" (TED Talks, 2011). Professor Ariely has encapsulated the conventional wisdom about the insurance industry, saying, "If you tried to create a system to bring out the worst in humans, it would look a lot like the insurance of today."

MAKING LEMONADE

This book is about a company called Lemonade, which set out to change the very dynamics of the insurer–insured relationship—or, rather, turn it back into what it once was. Assisted in this effort by the creation of cutting-edge technology, Lemonade soon became the darling of what was to be called InsurTech.

In the following pages, you will read about how this little company with a funny name came to be. How the company grew from an idea on a wall to the leading InsurTech company in the world in less than two years by creating a business model never quite seen in modern insurance.

And, along the way, you will see in no small part a personal journey on a man who climbed the corporate ladder of the modern insurance industry only to find its false foundation, forcing him to help create a new foundation for the industry and for himself.

Of course, I could know none of this on a totally ordinary day in April 2015 when I got what turned out to be the most important call of my life.

STORY 1:

An Ordinary Day

April 21, 2015, began as an ordinary Tuesday, with all the usual elements: the buzz of the 5 a.m. alarm, the aroma of dark-roast coffee from the corner Starbucks, the early ferry into the New York City and *The New York Times* headlines (mostly bad news) on my mobile—in short, another day in paradise.

Or was it purgatory?

Truth be told, my new insurance consultancy, Innovation Insurance Group LLC, founded just three years earlier, was booming. I had more clients than I needed to support my small office at the World Financial Center in New York and a small but nice apartment in Jersey City with a water view of Manhattan. At age fifty-seven and after three decades spent toiling in the insurance field, I was living the dream.

Or so I thought.

Little did I know that by 5 p.m. that day my entire life would change—all for an idea that had nothing more than a name of a popular summer beverage.

Let me explain. I'm Ty Sagalow, and unless you're involved with complex types of insurance, you've probably never heard of me. Then again, if you're in the industry, there is a good chance you have.

For almost my entire adult life, I was an inside man in insurance. Over the course of twenty-five years, I rose through the ranks at American International Group (AIG). It seemed like a lifetime. Then I went to Zurich Insurance for what I thought would be my golden years, but something wasn't right. I decided to strike out on my own, founding a consulting company I called Innovation Insurance Group. I wanted to see what could be done to make insurance work for people instead of against them. I'd spent my entire career in insurance helping my employer, usually a large corporate insurance company, and I'd made a decent amount of money doing so. Still, things felt off. The way I had lived my life didn't seem right somehow. So, I left that world to start my consulting company because I wanted to do something different. But was I actually doing anything different?

On this Tuesday morning, like the past Tuesday and all the Tuesdays before, I didn't feel that I was making a difference, not really. With my new venture, I was just continuing to work for big corporations in another way. I have never been religious, but I'm as spiritual as the next guy, so I remember wondering wistfully that morning as the ferry pulled in and I walked past homeless and hipster side by side, if somehow insurance could be part of the solution for our city. Could insurance be a vehicle to help communities, not as a side show but as part of its core purpose? I wondered, but, as usual, threw that idea into the recycle bin along with my empty cup and lid: paper, plastic.

Been there, dreamed that, I said to myself. Back in the 1990s, when I was publishing tomes on the impact insurance can play on corporate behavior, I'd philosophized that an insurance company could temper the era of Greed Is Good by using insurance rates to penalize antisocial behavior. By the new millennium, though, that dream had been crushed, just like my coffee cup was that morning.

Taxicab horns jolted me from my reverie. And so, my morning continued: the slow elevator to the thirtieth floor, more coffee from the Keurig machine, phone calls with clients, one after the other. That day was like every other: trying to build a business, make money, pay the bills.

During my third caffeine fix, my buzzing phone displayed an unfamiliar number. *Probably another eleventh-hour crisis*, I thought (coincidentally, as it happened to be 11 o'clock). I figured it was just another entrepreneur with another "great idea" but with neither the funds nor, if one were brutally honest, the ability to execute the idea. Alas, you never know who could be on the other end of the line, and so a good consultant always answers the phone. After all, who could know when the opportunity I was secretly looking for would knock? So I answered on the first ring.

"Hello, Mr. Sagalow?" The voice on the other end of the phone had a cultured British accent—not like this kid from Brooklyn. But I wasn't impressed yet. Who was this guy? And, as if reading my mind, he added, "You don't know me. I'm Daniel Schreiber. I'm calling from Tel Aviv. We googled 'insurance' and 'innovation.' Your name was the first, and really the only, one that came up."

"Yes, this is Ty. Good to meet you, Daniel." There was silence on the other end of the line, so I quickly added, "How can I help you?" (By the way, I was not surprised by the Google reference. Because I do zero advertising, most people find me by Google. I really owe them flowers.)

"Well, Ty," he continued, "my partner and I are looking for someone who can help with an innovative new insurance model we've invented for the new sharing economy. We're hopeful that it can work, but we're absolutely not insurance professionals. That's where you come in."

"Go on," I said.

Daniel continued. "We eventually want to launch worldwide, but we want to start with the US. We're based in Israel and don't know the US market that well. You seem to be an innovation leader there."

Ever since opening the practice, I'd been spending all my waking hours and too much of my sleeping hours, as my wife can attest, thinking of ways to help entrepreneurs launch new businesses where a new insurance product of some sort needed to be invented. It was nice for someone to notice.

To state the obvious, risks are constantly evolving in new ways, and insurance needs to stay ahead of them. For my entire career, I have been involved in innovation. At AIG, I created an insurance policy for the Y2K crisis and eventually became AIG's president of product development, a role I continued with other insurance companies. But in my new life, what I enjoyed most, and all too infrequently, was trying to help startup entrepreneurs, not big corporations, create something new.

"Okay, you've got my attention, Daniel. So what exactly is this idea of yours?"

"I can't tell you anything over the phone. It's highly confidential," came the reply.

This was a frustrating but not uncommon response. "Understood," I said. *But I can't know if I can help you if you don't tell me anything*, I thought but didn't say. Instead, my words were more lawyerly: "I will send over an NDA, but for now is there anything you can tell me? What's the name of your new idea?"

After a long pause, as if deciding whether he could trust me, Daniel told me: "Lemonade."

I can't say that I expected that.

"Lemonade," I repeated. (Always a good thing to do when you don't know what to say.)

"What's your schedule for the rest of the week?" Daniel asked. Once freed from the secrecy of the name, he seemed more relaxed. "I can come by and explain our idea. It shouldn't take more than two hours."

"I can give you an hour," came my reply. Although this guy had a nice British accent, I didn't know him from Adam. And I have learned the hard way that if it takes you more than an hour to explain your idea, it's no good. Besides, business development meetings aren't billable.

I agreed to see him the following week, on April 30, at 10:30 a.m. I noted in my calendar everything I knew about this new venture: "Israel company tech with insurance/sharing-economy idea," with only the vaguest idea of what lay ahead. I didn't even write down the word Lemonade. *That name will never stick*, I thought.

I ushered Daniel off the phone, telling him I looked forward to seeing him the next week. When I got home that night, my soon-to-be-wife, Jane, asked, "How was your day?"

"The usual," I said.

Boy, was I wrong.

STORY 2:

Meeting Daniel

When I hung up the phone with Daniel on April 22, 2015, I had no idea that, within forty days, I would be in Old Jerusalem to ink the deal of a lifetime. The days leading up to my life-changing Jerusalem visit were, in retrospect, the proverbial silence before the storm. Because following that first call with Daniel, the next nine days could not have been more ordinary.

So, by the time Thursday, April 30 rolled around, I was feeling about as adventurous as a long-term bond. I wasn't particularly excited about Daniel's visit, and in fact, I almost forgot about it until I saw it pop up on my Google calendar.

But my all-too-brief hour with Daniel changed all that.

At exactly 10:30 a.m. to the second, in walked a man who looked like a modern version of the silent screen-era heartthrob Rudolph Valentino—and who started off almost as silent. We exchanged a few pleasantries, but then he turned the focus to me: "Ty, tell me about yourself." It was the first time a founder of a startup did not want to immediately begin talking about himself (or herself) and his great new idea.

Not sure where the conversation was going, I told him about my business helping entrepreneurs. I rapidly went through the entrepreneurs I have helped launch companies, both before and after starting my own consulting firm. This included ventures such as creating bitcoin theft insurance so a new bitcoin exchange could attract new customers, intellectual property collateral insurance so an IP appraiser could get a leg up on his competition, and collectible authenticity insurance to help an entrepreneur steal eBay customers by promising each of its collectibles to be insured by Lloyds of London as being authentic. And, of course, I hedged my bet by underscoring my decades with traditional carriers like AIG and Zurich, including helping to invent cyber-risk and Y2K insurance.

After spending thirty minutes answering Daniel's questions, I seemed to have won him over. At least he was willing to talk about his idea for Lemonade. The first thing I noticed was that, despite being a lawyer and a technology executive, he stayed away from talking about either law or technology in describing his vision. Instead, he talked more from the point of view of an economist and sociologist. Society, he explained, was beginning to realize that goods and services can be shared among people instead of purchased from a centralized, and unfeeling, corporate entity. For example, the biggest hotel room renter, Airbnb, neither owned nor rented any real estate. The largest taxi company, Uber, did not own a single taxi cab. Communities are helping each other in every segment of society. Why not in insurance, too? Indeed, it should be happening more in insurance. We agreed: Everybody hates insurance. Despite clever commercials about hands holding hands and insurers being on your side, the essence of insurance as a community had all but disappeared.

Insurance had turned into a necessary evil instead of a social good.

It was during this initial conversation that Daniel answered a question in the back of my mind: Why the name Lemonade? "When life gives you lemons, make lemonade." It was about returning insurance to a social good. Now I got it. *Maybe the name will stick,* I thought with a shrug.

At the end of the hour, Daniel asked a simple question: "Do you think you can help us?" I honestly didn't know, and said so.

Daniel was impressive, clearly highly intelligent, and, although he admitted he had no expertise in insurance, I could tell by our conversation that he understood the fundamentals: People or their property are exposed to a risk of various kinds of loss; the insurer estimates the likelihood and extent of the losses (known as a frequency and severity analysis in industry-speak), and sets the proper rate for premiums to cover some or all of those losses. Clients pay premiums so that if the risk leads to a loss that is covered, the insurer will make them whole.

The traditional way that insurance makes money is by the insurer minimizing its risk of any single covered event by taking premiums from a wide group of people or corporations using the "Law of Large Numbers" to ensure that no single insured or event can get you in trouble. This is also called "spreading your risk," and it is key to profitability for insurance companies. After all, some people pay premiums but never suffer a covered loss (a payday for the insurer); some people pay premiums and suffer a covered loss in excess of the premiums (a loss to the insurer, unless the claim is denied). Insurance statistics show that only a minority of insureds suffers a loss. Thus, the many pay for the losses of the few. People with consistent good luck can't help but feel that the money they spend on insurance is money wasted.

Meanwhile, the more claims an insurer can successfully deny, the more money goes to the insurance company's bottom line. And, so, regardless of whether insurance carriers deny claims that they shouldn't, most of their customers believe they do. This is not to say that insurance people are inherently unethical; in fact, within the industry are many professional standards and honorable people, as well as a whole bunch of regulators who keep insurers in line and on the customer's side. Still, there is that inherent conflict of interest. And it is this conflict of interest, inherent in the very business model of modern insurance, which

Daniel thought he could fix. And, after talking to Daniel, I began to think so, too.

The more Daniel spoke the more I was intrigued by the notion of returning insurance to its roots. After all, I reasoned, that is how insurance began, many centuries ago, as a way of communities helping each other. This was before "big business" took over and created, or so it seemed to most people, an "us vs them" game of insured vs insurer.

Daniel wanted to change all that. What if the insurance risks as well as the returns were shared among insureds? The reality was that there were already many existing insurance business models that attempted to do exactly this, such as (for the insurance geek readers) Mutuals, Captives, Safety Groups, Reciprocals. The insurance industry already had many kinds of business models with the same goal as what Daniel was talking about. But were any of them really accomplishing the task at hand: eliminating the inherent conflict of interest while restoring faith between the insurance company and its customers? The truthful answer was "no." And, if not, could we really create a new model, perhaps somewhat modeled on the old, to do that? Could it work? Could I help?

Could insurance really be returned back to the community idea again? And if so, how could it be done? The notion raised a number of questions in my mind, and truthfully, I wondered if it was even possible. Besides, who would financially fund such a venture, where communities and not the insurance company's shareholders enjoyed much of the profits? There were ten questions to be answered for every one we discussed. And Daniel readily admitted that he had not thought of any of them. So, at the end of our hour, we parted with more questions than answers. I almost regretted that I didn't give him the two hours he originally asked for. At the same time, I wasn't sure he needed me or that I could really help.

"Can you come to Israel to spend time with me and my partner, Shai Wininger?" Daniel asked as he was leaving. Shai was the founder and CEO of a brilliant, Israel-based company called Fiverr, and he was one of those truly rare technologists who can code software and run a software company with equal expertise. Every bit as impressive as Daniel, I soon discovered that Shai could solve in minutes a problem that took established insurance companies months to figure out.

As for going to Israel, I was born a Jewish kid in Brooklyn. While not very religious, I was proud of my Jewish heritage and somewhat ashamed that I had never visited Israel. *A free trip to Israel? Why not?* I said, "Sure."

Daniel said he would consult with Shai and call me later. He walked away as I wondered whether I would, in fact, ever hear from him again.

Jerusalem

Ten minutes after Daniel left my office, he called me. "When in the next three weeks can you fly to Israel?" he asked. As I soon found out, if you deal with Israeli entrepreneurs, you had to be prepared to make quick decisions. Three weeks later, I was on a plane to Israel.

The day before I left for the trip, I had lunch with XL Innovate CEO Tom Hutton. XL, a large, global insurance carrier, was one of the first insurance companies to create a venture capital fund whose mission was to find innovative new companies which could help make XL successful. Tom is a brilliant executive and past CEO of an insurance company, and he has the unique ability to combine the best of insurance know-how with that of a top-flight venture capitalist. I told Tom that I was leaving for Israel the next day "to meet some tech company with an insurance idea." I also told him that, if I thought it was anything interesting, I would let him know. (Later, XL Innovate would lead the $13 million Series A round for Lemonade, and Tom would join the company's board of directors.)

On Thursday, May 14, 2015, I arrived in Tel Aviv for a meeting on Sunday. The workweek in Israel, as I found out, is Sunday to Thursday. After spending a good part of the weekend enjoying the beaches in Tel

Aviv, I taxied to Jerusalem early Sunday morning.

I was fully prepared to do business with Daniel on my first day there, but he would not hear of it. I had to see "the greatest city on earth," as he called it. The Old City in Jerusalem is really something to be seen. I saw myriad faces of every ethnicity going peacefully about the day in distinct neighborhoods—Jewish, Muslim, Christian, and Armenian—each secure in the knowledge that their God was with them.

It was Sunday, so church bells were pealing in the Christian quarter, but for Jews and Muslims, the Sabbath was over, and it was back to business, with colorful vendors conducting commerce in the shadow of sacred sights: the Western Wall for the Jews, the Al-Aqsa Mosque for the Muslims, and the Church of the Holy Sepulcher for Christian pilgrims, built on a spot believed to be the location of the crucifixion of Jesus, to name just a few holy spots. Yarmulke, cross, and Koran were all in view. This wasn't a place for just tepid tolerance for religion; it was a celebration of faiths—and there was history in every one of the pale pink stones shaping the cityscape.

Daniel was playing docent and explaining the history of Jerusalem. The most memorable story he told was about a ladder hanging from a window of the Church of the Holy Sepulcher. He pointed it out:

> *There it is! You see it, hanging there? Over time, the church was controlled by different sects, and they each had a portion of the building. Each sect would, from time to time, try to control a portion of the building controlled by another sect. This went on for hundreds of years. Ultimately, they decided to stop the mutual encroachment and agreed that everyone stay where they were. In fact, to hold the agreement firmly in place, nobody could move anything. Not a thing. On that day, the windows were being cleaned and the workers were using a ladder to reach a high window. But the deal was the deal. Nothing could be moved. So, the ladder is still there, four hundred years later.*

To this day, I call it Daniel's ladder.

Daniel could tell I could have heard a hundred more stories, but it was dinner time. "Let's get some hummus," he said. We went to the Arab quarter and found ourselves surrounded by men speaking Arabic, which, along with Modern Hebrew, was at the time of my visit an official language of Israel. I remember feeling a sudden rush of love and appreciation for Israel as I realized that here was a democracy that, by its own choice and out of respect for minority rights, elevated the language of a people, some of whom were dedicated to their annihilation, to the status of an official language standing side by side with their own. And here we were on that bright Sunday afternoon with those same people, supposed mutual enemies, eating with us side by side, in peace.

Hearing these stories and experiencing the sights and sounds of Zion, I was transported to my own Jewish roots, ones that I had never realized were so strong or so deep .

Alas, however, I was here on business and there was work to do.

STICKY NOTES

The next day, I met Dan's cofounder, Shai Wininger, also the company's chief technology officer. Having built a technology company doing hundreds of millions of dollars a year after only a handful of years, Shai was already itching for a new challenge.

So there we were, the three of us sitting in a room with a blank wall adorned by nothing more than eight letters: LEMONADE. That's all we had: the name of the company. We knew that it would have something to do with insurance and that it would take the industry back to its community core. And, of course, it would have technology that no one in the world had ever seen. That was it. Three core elements and a name. We had some work to do.

We started brainstorming with sticky notes. If one fluttered down to the floor, we kept going. We used up packs of the things. It was a marathon that lasted three days, almost nonstop.

First we had to figure out what type of insurance Lemonade would sell. In reality, that was an easy decision. Daniel wanted insurance that touched people rather than corporations. The first two types of insurance people buy are homeowner's insurance and automobile insurance. Automobile insurance is much more complicated to create than homeowner's insurance, and it requires a larger organization and relationships with repair shops, etc. Too much for a startup to accomplish. Plus, most auto insurance losses arise from lawsuits and other claims against the insured, while homeowner claims involve a direct loss of or damage to the insured's property, a space where Lemonade's to-be-created "behavioral economics" process would be most effective. Accordingly, somewhat directed but also somewhat by default, we decided to be in homeowner's. In reality, this also was the obvious choice for our target audience: Millennials. Soon it became obvious that our first product focus should be on the type of insurance Millennials first buy (or should first buy) after leaving home: renter's insurance.

We determined that Lemonade is actually two companies: an insurance company and a technology company. (Later we would add two more.) The insurance company—or would it be an insurance broker? Something to figure out later—would provide insurance to members of a community. The technology company would provide the technology and management support to the insurance company in exchange for a 20 percent fee. If there were profits from the insurance company, they would go back to the community members.

To make this work, we needed our community of insureds to trust us, and we needed to be worthy of that trust. In other words, we needed to change behavior—both ours and our policyholders'. Solving that big problem went on the list.

At the end of the third day in Israel, I sensed a change in the environment. What was once a blank wall now had dozens of different-colored stickies on it. Strong columns of like kind slowly began to emerge: underwriting, claims, distribution, product, technology, customer relationships.

Finally, fortysomething hours later, the buzzing settled down. You could hear a pin drop in the silence. Daniel and Shai sat next to each other on one side of our brainstorming table, around which they had been restlessly roaming only hours before. I sensed that something formal would be happening momentarily. And I was right.

It was Daniel who first spoke. "We think you're our guy."

"Thanks," I said, having actually no idea what he meant. "What do you mean?"

They smiled. "How does chief insurance officer sound?"

I knew these guys for three days, and they were ready to put their baby in my hands. Now I was smiling. "Wow," was the only reply I could think of.

But there was a catch. Funding. Money is always a catch.

"How much do you need to raise?" I asked.

"We need to raise $10 million in twelve weeks before we can launch," Daniel answered.

Calling that an ambitious goal in the difficult capital-raising economic environment of 2015 would be an understatement. "I'll tell you what, gentlemen," I said. "I'll work on a contract basis one day a week—no title necessary—until you get funding. At the end of the twelve weeks, you pay me no matter what. However, if you get the $10 million in twelve weeks, I will give up my consulting and be your guy."

Frankly, as great as the ideas were, I wasn't holding my breath on these guys getting the $10 million they needed. I knew more than anyone how closed-off and convoluted the insurance space can be, with its complex and strict regulatory structure being predisposed to deny entrance to new firms. What investor in his right mind would throw millions at a brand-new company—especially one with a radically new business model and a funny name?

It'll never happen, I thought, as I boarded the plane back to New York.

Who Are We?
(and Will Anyone Care?):
The Lemonade Business Model

As those first few funding weeks went by, fundamental questions kept popping into my head. Every startup begins with the same questions: Who are we? What is our purpose? And, possibly most important: Will anyone care? These were the questions we asked ourselves in those first few weeks and kept on asking for months and years to come. There was a strong debate among the founding members on the answers. We disagreed passionately about which aspect of this proposed new insurance model should be the most important.

In other words, what was the fundamental value proposition of Lemonade?

> **Should Lemonade be about *helping communities*?** —i.e., making the world a better place by devoting any excess premium to communities or charities? That was Daniel's driving passion. We were about community. The fact that we organized early on as a B Corp—i.e., a third-party certified

corporate structure devoted to a social purpose—emphasized that.[2]

- **Should Lemonade be about *changing behavior?***—i.e., eliminating the conflict of interest inherent to the modern insurance model? That was what most moved me.
- **Should Lemonade be about harnessing *technology?***—i.e., building anxiety-free, user-friendly applications and producing superior customer experience? That was Shai's vision.

Discussions about a company's fundamental value proposition have practical consequences, especially for marketing. This was no less true in the case of Lemonade. At first, we decided to emphasize Daniel's favored theme of community, and quickly referred to ourselves as a "peer-to-peer" insurance organization, capitalizing on a catchphrase at the time. By deciding to become a B Corp, we were emphasizing our focus on social and environmental accountability, among other things, in lieu of straight profits. While this might make it more difficult for us to raise capital in the future, the status went to the heart of what we believed Lemonade to be.

This identification became very popular among the industry press of the time, and we were called the leading "peer-to-peer insurance company." The "Uber of Insurance" was a frequent phrase. Peer-to-peer dovetailed into a central part of our business model. At the end of the insurance application process for new clients, which we called onboarding, we would ask the applicant to choose his or her favorite charity from a list of about fifteen. We would then group applicants by

---

2   As explained by B Lab, which certifies these types of entities, B Corps are for-profit companies certified to meet rigorous standards of "social and environmental performance, accountability, and transparency"—i.e. for-profits committed to making the world a better place. And, as B Lab notes, there is a growing community of more than 2,100 Certified B Corps from 50 countries and over 130 industries working together toward one unifying goal: to redline success in business. See https://bcorporation.net/ for more information.

choice of charity, creating virtual peer groups of like-minded insureds who would rise or fall based on their individual group performance regardless of the performance of any other group (that's where the peer-to-peer concept comes in.)

We theorized that this approach would have at least two major benefits. First, charities would receive the benefit of profitable groups thus fullfilling our mission to try to make the world a better place. Second, we believed, or at least hoped, that knowing that any unclaimed monies would go to charity (and not just any charity but the one chosen by the policyholder) and not to the insurance company would make our policyholders less likely to "fudge" (to use a nice term) on claims. Indeed, perhaps, knowing that denying covered claims would not increase our profits one bit but rather rob money from charities might even change our claims behavior. (More on Lemonde's theory of Behavioral Economics later.)

Having established the various peer groups, we decided we would operate like a Software As a Service (SAAS) technology company, taking a flat fee to run all the insurance operations. To be more specific, for every dollar in premium, we would take our flat fee, 20 percent at the time. Next we would buy reinsurance (insurance that insurance companies buy) for another around 20 percent, and then we would set aside an additional rainy-day fund for future claims and emergencies for another 20 percent.

At that point, with 40 percent of the premium left to go, things got interesting. First, of course, that would be used to pay current claims. What if current claims and losses did not need the entire 40 percent? Although traditional insurance carriers typically keep for themselves the leftover (i.e., excess) money not spent on expenses or paid in claims, we gave 100 percent of those unearned monies back to the charity chosen by the group. We called it the Annual GiveBack, and it happened every July. We analyzed each group separately so that if a particular group of policyholders had a good year, 100 percent of the excess monies would go their chosen charity, regardless of how well or poorly other groups did. To me, peer-to-peer conceptualized all of that. However, we discovered that, although this made us popular with the media, which was able to compare Lemonade to other peer-to-peer companies like Uber and Airbnb, the reference did not resonate with our customers, who wanted a clearer picture of exactly what our value proposition was to them. Because the most important view is always the one taken by your customers, we eventually changed our tagline or identification into an emphasis on technology and behavior. Our new descriptor emphasized that we had created a new kind of insurance company "based on behavioral economics and AI."

Honestly, when we decided to change this identifying characteristic it was something of a sad moment for me, as I thought that the new emphasis would stray from our commitment to community. However, I realized that everything would be fine: Instead of *talking* about helping communities, we simply *did it*.

All companies have some sort of value proposition. In my mind, a company can be considered a "good" company even if it does what other companies do, but does it better. Almost all "good" companies fall into this category and, truth be told, one can make a lot of money simply by being better than the competition at the same game. But *great* companies are different than that. Great companies are more than imitators, implementers, streamliners, or multipliers. Great companies do something new and unique. Lemonade's proposition was new and unique. It sought to completely change the business model of a trillion-dollar industry by creating a whole new way of conducting business. If successful, Lemonade would become not just a "good" company but a great one.

At least, that was the theory back in Summer 2015. Now if we could just find someone who was willing to put up millions of dollars to test that theory. Daniel and Shai focused on raising those millions of dollars to test our proposition while I parachuted into meetings when needed.

It's never easy for a startup to raise capital, and, in our case, I feared that it would be next to impossible: We had no financial statements, no organizational chart, and no product. Just an idea, really. Most startups that attract major capital have something: a proof-of-concept widget, a pre-existing customer base, a technology platform, a biotech patent, something. We had nothing but a PowerPoint, with concepts generated from our wall of sticky notes in Jerusalem.

We knew it would be far easier to raise capital if we were planning to be an insurance broker, the middleman between the seller of insurance, the insurance carrier, and the buyer of insurance, the insured. An insurance broker might need only a couple of million dollars or less to start operations. But an insurance carrier, what we wanted to be (see sidebar below), needed much more capital—at least $10 million. What's more is that the money would just sit there in a capital reserve account earning virtually no interest. Most VCs, I reasoned, would run the other way if confronted with such a deal.

Imagine my surprise, then, when renowned venture capitalist Michael Eisenberg of Aleph, one of the VCs behind WeWorks and other top technology companies, put down our first millions: $6.5 million, to be exact. This amazing contribution from a man who has made such a difference in Israel changed everything for us. Michael was known for being smart and quick to see the right opportunity. That meant others might follow. Sure enough, not before long, we also heard from none other than Sequoia Capital. When Daniel told me this, he didn't even bother explaining who Sequoia was; that would have insulted my intelligence: Sequoia had bankrolled a fifth of all the companies on Nasdaq, from Apple to Instagram to PayPal, and everybody knew it. (Everybody but me, that is. I'm an old insurance guy. What do I know about venture capital?) I was too embarrassed to ask, "Sequoia who?" But when I looked it up that night, I knew that we had truly made it big with a capital B. I spoke to a couple of friends in Silicon Valley. One said "Ty, there are people who wait their whole lives to get a call from Sequoia."

So, days later, there I was representing Lemonade in a meeting with six managing directors from Sequoia Capital. Daniel gave me a warning. "Ty," he said, "Shai and I have done our part, but if they don't like you, there will be no deal." No pressure.

Fortunately, they were smart enough—or I was lucky enough—that they asked me about things I knew, so I had plenty to say. But then came the tough question. "Ty, you have a successful business. Why join a startup?" I answered without hesitation: "It's not because Lemonade is a billion-dollar idea." (Back then I thought a billion-dollar idea was a lot of money.) "It's because of Daniel and Shai." I was referring to their track record of getting things done.

Then it was my turn to ask question. I asked only one: "Why do you want to make this investment? You haven't really ever invested in insurance with its large capital requirements. Why now?" Echoing my own words, they simply said, "Daniel and Shai." (Years later, Tom Hutton similarly would tell me that XL's decision to lead the early A round was more due to its confidence in Daniel and Shai than their confidence in the new Lemonade model.)

The deal was on. Sequoia matched Michael's investment, and suddenly we had $13 million in the bank. We were on our way.

Within twelve weeks, Lemonade had successfully raised a multi-million-dollar seed round led by Sequoia Capital and Aleph. It was the largest seed financing Sequoia had ever invested, the largest seed round in the history of Israel, and the largest seed in the entire technology sector worldwide in 2015. Wow!

On August 1, 2015, yours truly and business development vice president Maya Prosor proudly opened a small office at 85 Broad Street in New York's Financial District while Daniel and Shai were working in Israel along with Shai's brilliant prodigy, Moshe Lieberman. (More about Maya and Moshe later.)

Insurance Broker or Carrier

The first Big Decision—Insurance Broker or Carrier. We had begun Lemonade with a fundamental decision to make, whether we should be an insurance broker or an insurance carrier. It may sound like a minor question, but it isn't. An insurance broker is the middleman between the seller (i.e., the insurance carrier) and the buyer (i.e., the insured). For a startup, there are a lot of advantages to becoming an insurance broker: less expensive to build (thus less funding needed), less regulation and less or no underwriting risk (i .e . the risk that losses and expenses paid out will exceed premium received.) Thus, it is perhaps not surprising that choosing to become an insurance broker was the universal advice of our high-powered advisors. "Don't try to create a whole new insurance carrier," they told us. "Being a broker is so much easier," they said. "It doesn't take much money, it carries no insurance risk, and there's no need to hire underwriters. You're a middleman. There's also far less regulation and much easier licensing. You don't need to create products; you only need to sell them."

However, this advice did not strike the right cord with Daniel, Shai, and me. It would mean that we would have to find an insurance carrier willing to go along with our new business model and one that could, in theory, pull out at any time if they believed things were not going well. In other words, we would be putting our fate into the hands of another.

So, after going 'round and 'round on the issue, I asked our highly paid advisor why he felt so strongly that Lemonade should be an insurance broker and not an insurance carrier. He blurted out an answer: "We have many clients going in this direction, and none going in the direction you want, Ty. We can use the same research we do for you and our other clients," he told me.

The minute he said it, he knew that he had put his foot in his mouth. By telling me that his real interest was getting paid multiple times for the same work—a typical consultant's strategy—it let out that he was putting his own needs before ours, and asking us to be just like everyone else to boot. But to this day, I am grateful for the *faux pas*. Something clicked for me, and I smiled politely and said, "I think the decision has just been made." We would take the road not taken and become a fully independent, regulated, and licensed insurance carrier in control of our own destiny. It would turn out to be the most important decision Lemonade ever made.

$13 Million and Six People

Now that we had money from Sequoia and Aleph, the real work began. We had accepted Other People's Money, and with that, the burden of responsibility. The receipt of funds made us a financial company with consummate responsibilities under state and federal laws. Moreover, our investors expected a return—and a big one at that, given their track record.

For a split second, I was almost disappointed at the rapid success in fundraising. The visionary in me wanted just one more day of brainstorming with sticky notes; the financial conservative in me wanted to go out and get more millions before buckling down; the kid in me just wanted to go back to see Daniel's Ladder. But there was no time for any of that. We had to craft from scratch a type of insurance company never before created in the history of insurance and disrupt a trillion-dollar industry.

No pressure.

THE SIX FOUNDING MEMBERS

Lemonade had six founding members. I've already told you about Daniel and Shai, the two Founders, and of course, you know about me. But what about the other three? Two came in the form of two top-drawer people Daniel and Shai had brought along, and the third was a globally recognized leading figure in the area of behavioral economics.

Daniel brought Maya Prosor, who, as the head of business development at Powermat, reported to Daniel when he was President. Shai brought Moshe Lieberman, a young but incredibly talented software coder.

BUSINESS DEVELOPMENT

Business development was a key priority. We could build the greatest product in the world, but with no brokers or agents, and without a multimillion-dollar advertising campaign, how would people even know Lemonade insurance existed? Once they did learn about us, how would they react? "Will the dog eat the dog food?" was a foundational question for us—and one not easily answered.

The chief business development officer would have a tough job. The essence of Lemonade was to go directly to consumers, with no brokers as middlemen. This would require a mental shift for most consumers, who were used to dealing with a local insurance agent. Most large insurers, such as State Farm and Allstate, worked only through an internal agency force. There was one notable exception: GEICO, which had invented the direct-to-consumer model.

But that model didn't come cheaply. To replace the thousands of brokers and agencies that sell home and auto insurance, GEICO spends billions of dollars a year in television advertising. We needed to accomplish the same broker-free result without going on TV. For one thing, we didn't have the money (most of the funds we had collected had to go into reserve capital, by law). In addition, we didn't want to take GEICO head-on in TV land. As we often said, "If you are going to challenge Bobby Fischer to a game, don't make it chess." And GEICO was the Bobby Fischer of insurance television advertising.

Luckily, there was Maya Prosor.

Maya had been a right hand for Daniel when he was CEO of Powermat, a top Silicon Valley technology company whose wireless charging technology became the model for all similar products to come. She was the perfect candidate: wicked smart, charismatic, generous in spirit. With her blonde hair, blue eyes, and diminutive frame, she brought out my protective instincts at first. (I remember opening a door for her at some point, but then felt a little silly.) But I soon realized that she was tough as nails—all in all, everything we needed.

Daniel couldn't say enough good things about Maya. And vice versa. When I asked Maya why she was leaving a great job at a highly successful established technology company to work for a startup, she answered in one word: "Daniel."

For business development, we needed someone who could sell not only something intangible but also something nonexistent—i.e., something in the very process of being created. Who had heard of wireless mobile chargers before Powermat? Maya had put that product on the map, signing deals with dozens of companies, including building in a Powermat charger in Starbucks in California and New York. But could she translate that ability into insurance, something of which she had absolutely no knowledge or prior experience?

Maya's answer: Forget about seeking individual sales. Instead seek out groups such as real estate property owners who could be used as a distribution channel to their renters, as well as PTAs, churches, and communities that also could be used as distribution channels to their members. So-called affinity marketing—i.e., the use of associations or groups to distribute your insurance policy to their members—was not new; associations such AARP or the American Bar Association have had partnerships with insurance carriers for decades. But seeking the types of communities Lemonade wanted to reach out to as your affiliated associations was new.

As it turned out, not everyone wanted to dance with us. We had to abandon one of our most cherished hopes: to promote the annual GiveBack to charities through the charities themselves: PTAs, churches, synagogues, etc. We'd had a kind of pie-in-the-sky idea that we would knock on their doors to talk about our plan to give back our profits to them. Our pitch: If they could help us introduce Lemonade insurance to their members, they could get that new baseball diamond or new roof they needed with their share of the profits. But within six months, we realized that we had no market there. PTAs and the like were not used to talking to members about financial decisions. As Maya pointed out, we had to know when to give up. We knew Startup Lesson 1: *Don't be afraid to give up some of your dreams.* So, we abandoned that particular dream and never looked back.

Real estate property owners and managers were another story, however. They were frustrated that so many of their renters did not buy renter's insurance—despite the fact that the lease required it. A large portion of renters in New York, for example, are in their twenties and early thirties, part of the so-called Millennial Generation. Real estate property owners and managers complained that their Millennial renters did not buy renter's insurance because the insurance industry made it was so difficult to buy insurance. These renters did not want to waste time going to their local insurance brokers and simply could not figure out why buying a renter's policy should be any different from buying a couch on Amazon. Their frustration was understandable. The reason they couldn't understand why buying a renter's insurance policy wasn't as simple as making an Amazon Prime purchase is because it shouldn't be. That's where Shai's genius came in. He, Moshe, and our team developed their own software code enabling the purchase of renter's insurance in less than three minutes on any Apple or Android device. Lemonade solved the Millennial renter's problem and thus the property manager's problem. It was an instant success.

Capitalizing on this aspect of the business, Maya hired a team of people as business development managers. She led the team in forming dozens of partnerships with real estate companies and property owners, among others. Before long, and thanks to Maya, we had easy and friendly electronic access to literally hundreds of thousands of renters and homeowners who needed insurance.

TECHNOLOGY AND CODING

My grandmother used to say that if you wanted to make chicken soup, the first thing you need to find is a chicken. If we were building a technology company (which just happened to be an insurance company), the first thing we needed was technology. We needed a platform for all of us to stand on.

At first, we went to the usual players, those companies which created insurance platforms for underwriting, claims, premium billing, and policy administration for decades. They were well established in the market, and they were expensive. I remember one particular pitch meeting during which the platform vendor described how it could solve all of our technology problems for only a "few million dollars" and have us ready to go in "about one to two years." Shai leaned over to me and said, "Ty, I don't understand. I can build this in ninety days for one tenth of the price. What am I missing?"

I replied, "Nothing. You are not missing anything at all." At that moment, we decided to build our own technology.

To do that, we needed someone to lead that effort. Luckily, we had Moshe.

Shai had (and continues to have) an unparalleled reputation in Israel and around the world. A brilliant coder in his own right, he can lead dozens of young software technologists to heights they never could have imagined. And the best and brightest of them was Moshe Lieberman.

Moshe was a young coder (twenty-five or so) from Israel. We

needed him to build a system that would automate insurance claims while complying to the letter with insurance regulations.

It was several months before I met Moshe in person, as he was working out of Israel and I was based in New York. But working together via Slack, a newer technology that facilitates internet-based conversations, it was as if he was in the next room. His main work from Day 1 was to do the coding of our forms and rates from the Insurance Services Organization (ISO), an insurance membership group that provided sample policy forms and claims loss information to new insurance companies like us.

Two stories tell volumes about Moshe and why, without him, Lemonade would not have been a success as quickly as it was.

One day, I had a desperate need that only Moshe could fill. It was down to the last two days for form and license approval with the New York State insurance department, technically called the New York State Department of Financial Services, and they wanted us to make substantial changes in our policies before they could be approved. I called Moshe and explained the situation. He said, "Ty, I'm driving a car right now. I can't get to this right away. It is going to have to wait until I get home and then it is going to take a while."

I said, "How long, Moshe?"

His answer: "Pretty long. A full ten minutes." And he wasn't kidding: To Moshe, ten minutes is a long time.

Another time I called Moshe to request amendments to our basic policy form. We wanted to calculate the charge that people would pay for insuring an expensive piece of jewelry, and we needed to make about a dozen other changes. He said, "Okay. What are the changes?" I rattled them off with lightning speed, and all the while I could hear him typing on a keyboard. I figured he was taking notes and would work on the changes during the next few days. "Moshe," I said, "do you have all of that? Have you made notes all of it?"

He said, "No, Ty."

I demanded, "For God sake, Moshe, why not?"

He replied, "I made the changes while you were speaking. Was that the wrong thing to do? Should I unmake them?"

"No, Moshe, you shouldn't," I said.

And I never questioned Moshe again. Moshe had transformed the policy while we were talking. No memos, emails, or meetings as the months dragged by. Just a five-minute call and it was done. That's what a world-class coder can do.

Interestingly, Moshe also became a good underwriter. He could look at an ISO rating document and not only put it in code but also understand the underwriting foundations that led to the code.

Behavior Economics

If Lemonade was going to succeed, we needed to change behavior. So-called "Insurance Fraud" costs the industry billions of dollars a year. Otherwise law abiding citizens feel it is "OK" to "fudge" on their insurance claims. We believed that the reason for this laid at the fault of the insurance industry and an insurance model which rewarded insurance companies every time a claim was denied. So, if we were to change the behavior of our customers we needed to begin with ourselves. But how?

One of the world's greatest minds in the discipline known as "Behavior Economics" is Professor Dan Ariely, the James B. Duke Professor of Psychology and Behavioral Economics at Duke University. Professor Ariely, also an Israeli, has written and spoken about why people stretch the truth and when. More importantly, he has counseled on what changes can be made to lessen this effect. So, it is not surprising that soon Daniel and Professor Ariely were brought together. What did the professor say when Daniel asked what he thought about insurance from a behavioral economics point of view? "If you wanted to invent something that brings out the worst in human nature, you couldn't find anything better than insurance."

Dan Ariely would become Lemonade's chief behavioral officer and its final founding member.

THE FOUNDING SIX

So, there we were, the six founding members: Daniel and Shai, the two founders, Maya, Moshe, Dan Ariely and me: five Israelis and a Jew from Brooklyn who had never seen Jerusalem until a little company called Lemonade changed his life.

And this was just the beginning.

STORY 6:

Building the Team

So now it was time to build the team around the founding six. My task was to create the insurance operations—i.e., essentially to form an insurance company from scratch, with one person per function. It was critical to find the right people. We needed people who had decades of experience but were brave enough to work for a startup. "Midlife crisis" was the phrase Daniel used, and it was the right one. We were looking for a few good men and women probably over age thirty-five (i.e., about the time we begin to realize that we won't live forever), highly successful in the traditional insurance community, and ready—indeed, anxious—to move on to something completely new and untested.

I had a short shopping list of positions I needed to fill for the insurance operations, much like a grocery list with orange juice, milk, bread, and butter:

- chief underwriting officer
- chief claims officer
- chief financial officer
- chief legal officer
- chief operations officer

My mission: Find the most talented senior insurance professionals out there who wanted to give it all up for a startup with almost no people, very little money (comparably speaking), no track record, and no license to operate or even any guarantee to ever have one. Executive recruiters told us it could take years. I gave myself four months.

I couldn't imagine anything more fun.

UNDERWRITING

Finding a chief underwriting officer was my first challenge. The heart of any insurance company lies in its underwriters. These are the people who must determine the right price and the right terms for the right risk. Underwriting professionals tend to be traditional folks—and the more years they put in, the more conservative they typically become. You would, too, if you spent your time gazing at actuarial tables and conducting statistical regressions.

I had given myself four months to find not just an underwriter but also the right people for claims, finance, and legal. Within four weeks, I had found a great candidate for the first category. Rob Giurlando was a former chief underwriting officer who had experience with a homeowner's insurance product at two major insurance companies specializing in high-net-worth customers. I invited him to meet me at Goldberg's Famous Deli in Millburn, New Jersey, where, over a roast beef sandwich and a knish, he told me his story.

Rob had a traditional Italian look about him: medium build with dark hair and an easy smile. He was the type of person one immediately liked. And he'd had it with the insurance industry. He found the old way of doing things frustrating, too often done without sufficient understanding of customer needs. He was planning to take early retirement from insurance and to become a high school history teacher. There was that crisis point I was looking for. I met him at Goldberg's with a mission in hand: to convince Rob to put his new career on hold and give insurance one more chance. I succeeded. Rob became Lemonade's first chief underwriting officer.

The job of a chief underwriting officer is to create an underwriting protocol for the evaluation of insurance risk. An insurance company gathers information such as credit scores and property information from its applicants and from third-party sources. Using that information, the insurer makes decisions as to which risks to accept and under what terms and premiums.

While Lemonade was a new insurance company, that did not mean Rob would have to start from scratch in creating rules for underwriting and accepting risks.

As mentioned, there's a little-known secret for startup insurance success called the Insurance Services Organization (ISO). (I have long ignored their official name change to Verisk in 2009, preferring to use is pre-merger, more historical, name.) It's a wonderful organization for new insurance companies like Lemonade. Based on work with actuaries, reinsurance companies, and rating agencies, ISO is an advisory and rating organization for the property casualty insurance industry which provides sample forms, estimates of "loss costs," (which can then be converted into premium ranges and potential rates), etc.—literally almost everything a new insurance company might want.

Alas, after only a short few months, Rob left Lemonade and pursued his dream of being a history teacher, but I will always be appreciative for the work he did for us at the beginning.

With Rob's departure, my job of finding a chief underwriting officer recommenced. Lemonade had already begun to hit the headlines, and, as it turned out, we had many qualified candidates. However, best among them was a former chief underwriting officer at Liberty Mutual, a former McKinsey partner, and a former actuary fellow, John Peters. John was the perfect candidate. As the months and years went on, John played an increasingly critical role at Lemonade. Smart, polished, and practical, John helped shape the entire insurance operations, and he was my (and Daniel's) choice to take over my role as chief insurance officer when I eventually left the day-to-day operations of Lemonade, leaving the insurance operations of the company in great hands.

CLAIMS

If the heart of an insurance company is underwriting, then its soul is claims. The Urban Dictionary defines the insurance industry as an industry which "makes promises to people to pay later that are never fulfilled." While there are exceptions to the rule, in general, claims people are trained to be cautious about paying claims. It is not that claims people are bad people. Indeed, the ones I know honestly wish to pay every covered claim as soon as possible. Of course, the claim has to be covered, and therein lies the rub.

No one would argue, I think, with the proposition that insurance carriers should resist paying uncovered claims, as such payments would result only in higher premiums for everyone. However, as the Urban Dictionary so well accounts, most insureds believe that carriers take this resistance a bit too far, delaying or denying every claim with the goal of paying as little as possible for as long as possible. After all, every dollar not paid in a claim is another dollar of profit for the insurance company. My job: to find a senior, experienced claims executive who thought differently.

Jim Hageman had more than twenty-five years of insurance claims experience, including extensive time in senior claims roles at such notable insurance companies as Progressive, The Hartford, and ACE, where he was head of personal lines claims, meaning claims for insurance sold to people—such as auto and homeowner's—as opposed to corporations. Tall and energetic, a volunteer with his local fire department as an emergency medical tech, he's your typical Connecticut Yankee type. Jim was tired of the old way of doing business and didn't hesitate to express his views. He agreed with me that there was an inherent conflict of interest between traditional insurers and their policyholders. Like the rest of us at Lemonade, he wanted a better way. It didn't take much to convince him that Lemonade was that way.

By the time we hired Jim, we had set up our physical office. It was an open format in a startup real estate company called WeWork (itself a Silicon Valley unicorn). Location: Financial District, New York. (Lemonade would later move to the much more hip Soho neighborhood.) A roof and four walls stretching far and wide, with no office doors or cubicle walls, it was something between a parking garage and an artist's loft. We loved it. Seeing nothing but windows, tables, and chairs on Day 1, Jim went to one of the open employee spaces facing a large window and wrote in large letters that he would never erase:

IT'S NOT OUR MONEY

Jim didn't have to explain his message to us—or to anyone who visited the offices in those days. These four simple words reminded him every day that Lemonade is merely a temporary custodian of the insured's funds. After our fees and expenses, all Lemonade's money goes back to the insureds in payment of losses, and if there is money left over, that goes to the charity of their choice. If we pay claims that are not covered, we are hurting the charities that our insureds want us to support. If we resist paying covered claims, we abandon the very essence of our promise to our insureds to be different. Balancing these is tricky, and Jim does it masterfully every day.

FINANCE

In a sense, insurance is all about money. Money comes in as premium and goes out as losses and expenses (and, in Lemonade's case, charitable contributions). The nuts and bolts of an insurance company is finance, and its chief financial officer is its master.

Finding the right CFO was in some ways the hardest job of all. If there is any area where it is difficult to find people who think out of the box, it has to be insurance finance. It has not changed for literally decades (some might even say for centuries). We had to find someone who knew the mold like the back of his hand but who also knew where and how it could be broken. In Fall 2015, we found that someone.

Ronald Topping had been laboring away at various AIG financial positions for a decade and a half. Funny thing, I was there during the same time and we even met once when Ron was chief financial officer of AIG Small Business, but we didn't remember each other. We were both too busy in our own sandboxes. Now Ron and I had a chance to work together, and I knew we would succeed. He was hired in December 2015—a great holiday present.

After he had left AIG, he had begun to help insurance companies that had gone bust and were in receivership. It doesn't get more arcane than that. So we knew he could meet a challenge, and we certainly had one for him. It's important to understand that, above everything else, insurance regulators expect an insurance company to have its financial house in order, to be able to answer any question at any time, and to produce any report showing every dollar in and every dollar out. Failure to perform means more than just losing your license; it could lead to time in jail.

Ron Topping stands at 6 foot 3 inches and weighs in at 275 pounds, a giant of a man in more than one respect. Ron embraced the InsurTech culture of Lemonade like no other, even to the point of wearing shorts to work during the summer months, a firm abandonment of the required dress code at AIG. Both New Jerseyites, Ron and I quickly became close friends, and we used to walk to the Wall Street–Hoboken ferry together. But behind that slaphappy look he cultivated, when it came to finance, Ron took no prisoners and insisted that Lemonade walked the straight and narrow, keeping all of us, including me, in line.

This wasn't always easy. Ron had a tough job because he truly had to start from scratch. He came into Lemonade, a company not only with no financial reports, but also with no financial reporting system. Welcome to the world of a startup! To support his work, he had at his disposal just a few Israeli coders, none of whom knew anything about insurance financial reporting.

He realized the challenge early on when he asked for a report on premiums earned for a past quarter and learned that we had no such report. In fact, we had no past data at all. (We eventually got the report we needed and made it retroactive.) Once again, we had interviewed vendors who said they could provide all the financial reports we needed, when we needed them and how we needed them. Once again, none had the speed or adaptability that we needed. We had to do it ourselves.

So, by sheer force of will if nothing else, Ron got what he needed: a working financial accounting system that any carrier would be proud of. Indeed, from time to time, we are asked to license our financial and underwriting systems. So far, we have always declined.

Legal

Insurance is a highly regulated industry. Our obligations are legal obligations arising from legal contracts. Before we bat an eye or move a muscle, we have to get a license permitting us to operate as an insurance carrier. Getting an insurer's license is not easy (remember the advice we got to become a broker). It takes time, money, and luck. There are mountains of regulatory requirements and hurdles designed to prevent insurance startups from doing the very thing Lemonade was trying to do. We needed a regulatory attorney—ASAP—and not just a good one but a great one. In other words, we needed another genius.

I'm a lawyer, and, I have to tell you, I really don't like lawyers. Lawyers generally tend to be fixed in their thinking, and insurance lawyers in some ways are the worst of the bunch. Creativity and the law do not necessary go well together, especially in insurance, a field which has not changed fundamentally in hundreds of years.

My goal was to find a lawyer who had both decades of experience in insurance law and strong relationships with major regulators throughout the country. At the same time, we needed someone who was highly creative and ready to go on a new adventure with a startup that might be out of business in a year. Our lawyer had to be going through a midlife crisis—someone ready for a new challenge. In other words, we were looking for someone I was pretty sure didn't exist.

I asked all the lawyers I knew what colleague they would recommend, and time and again, the answer came back to a single individual: Bill Latza. Bill was a partner turned "of counsel" in the well-known law firm of Stroock & Stroock & Lavan, one of the mighty insurance regulatory firms headquartered in New York City. So I went to Bill in August 2015 and saw a man who could have come out of Central Casting as the Man in the Gray Flannel Suit. Tall, thin, and gray-haired, he looked every inch the lawyer. I spoke to him about a new company called Lemonade—and to my surprise and glee, his eyes literally twinkled. As it turned out, Bill was having a midlife crisis of his own. He was seriously thinking about leaving the law, having been a practicing attorney for more than thirty-five years. Lemonade, he later confessed to me, convinced him to stick to practicing law. He signed on to be our outside counsel and, through his genius and reputation, he steered us through the many legal obstacles to come to become the first InsurTech insurance carrier. (A year later, when we decided we had grown up enough to have our own in-house general counsel, we offered Bill the job. He left Stroock & Stroock & Lavan and accepted the offer.)

BUSINESS OPERATIONS

In every company, there is one person who actually makes sure things get done. For Lemonade, that was Yael Cohen. Yael came to us from TASC Consulting, the Israeli version of McKinsey & Company, where she was a star. At Lemonade, it was one of Yael's many jobs to make sure the team and I accomplished what we needed to accomplish when we needed to. But to say that Yael was in charge of product management is like saying that Babe Ruth was in charge of running around the baseball field. In other words, no term, description, or title can do justice to what Yael did for me and the entire team at Lemonade. (For example, she did not just use the software program for managing all the necessary projects for Lemonade, she *created it*.) If we were in corporate America, she might have had the title of Chief Operations Officer, but for me, she was simply my savior.

Now we had our team of eleven[3]* players, ready to take on the world.

---

3   In reality, I wish I could go on and write something about each of the truly wonderful and brilliant people who were there at Lemonade in the first two years. My apologies that due to time and length restraints I was unable to do so and so, somewhat artificially, I stopped at the first eleven.

Daniel's Ladder

Ty's first conversation with Shai on insurance (note Shai's confused look), Israel

Shai's first conversation with Ty on technology (note Ty's confused look)

Creating the concept of Lemonade through yellow stickies

Ty agrees to help form Lemonade (May 2015, Israel)

The First Three

Ty works on the Lemonade Model

Shai whiteboarding claims flow

Ty, Daniel and Maya first meeting (at Starbucks, of course)

Lemonade's first home: 85 Broad Street, NYC

And Then There Were Six

Brainstorming the user experience

The First Core Team

Our first visit to New York Department of Financial Services (notice the suits)

85 Broad Street, busy at work (note Ron in shorts)

A Customer Service Request (note the thoughtful looks)

Off to Bermuda to see potential reinsurers

*Ajit Jain, Vice Chair,
Berkshire Hathaway
and Ty Sagalow
(He came to us!)*

Greg Hendricks (XL) whiteboarding new Lemonade reinsurance model

Ty and Dan Ariely

Ron and Ty (just another fun day in the office) 2 points for figuring out that the T-Shirt is sayiing "Shai" backwards.

Lemonade – The First 21

Celebrating New York,
Our first license
(Sept 2016)

Al Redmer, Jr.
@al_redmer

The insurance industry is ripe for disruption by technology. Listening to @daschreiber of Lemonade_inc. Lemonade will be in MD soon #naic

2:31pm · 12 Feb 2017 · Twitter for iPhone

Maryland Insurance Commissioner wants Lemonade

NAIC presentation

Jillian Froment   12:08 ⋮
to Daniel

Excellent presentation at the NAIC conference yesterday.
On behalf of the Ohio Department of Insurance, we'd love
to talk to you about your plans for Ohio.

Jillian Froment
Deputy Director
Ohio Department of Insurance
Jillian.Froment@insurance.ohio.gov

   Not interested

View Jillian's LinkedIn profile

Ohio Insurance Commissioner wants Lemonade too

AdvertisingAge

State Farm Wants You to be a Good Neighbor Too

By Adrianne Pasquarelli. Published on March 13, 2017.

The Bloomington, Ill.-based marketer, the largest auto insurer in the U.S., is debuting its Neighborhood of Good platform, which will connect consumers to charitable opportunities in their towns... To compete with a bevy of other players, which increasingly include more startup players like home insurer Lemonade, State Farm has been refreshing its marketing image.

State Farm Reacts to Lemonade Startup

...you might get stuck with a lemon.

Make the reliable choice — choose State Farm. With auto insurance, it pays to compare apples to apples. Many of our competitors advertise lower rates, but they may come at a big price if you don't get the service, coverage, or protection you need.

Don't get stuck with a lemon when it comes to your auto insurance. Let me show you what State Farm offers — including all the discounts and coverage options available to you. For a custom quote just call, email, or stop by.

Sincerely,

Anthony J. Ventresca

StateFarm

A Ventresca Ins Agy Inc
3001 Highway 27
Franklin Park, NJ 08823-1229
Bus: (732) 297-9037 Fax: (732) 297-6430
e-mail: tony@tonyventresca.com

Bridgewater NJ 08807-1843

State Farm Reacts to Lemonade Startup

What's Covered

FIRE AND SMOKE

A faulty Christmas light or your attempt at deep frying can cause some smoke and fire damage. We cover you for both.

CRIME AND VANDALISM

Your home is full of stuff: furniture, clothing, appliances. We cover you if any of it is stolen or damaged.

BAD WEATHER

Wind, lightning, and hail are scary. You're covered for all of them. Flood insurance isn't part of the basic policy.

Included with Coverage

Fire & Smoke

Sometimes that romantic candlelight evening ends with a visit from the fire brigade. Fear not! If your stuff catches fire or gets that indelible "eau de house fire" smell - we cover you for both smoke and fire damage.

Theft & Vandalism

If your stuff gets stolen or (somehow even more frustrating) gets needlessly destroyed, don't worry — you're covered. Go back to eyeing your neighbors suspiciously.

Weather

Lightning! Wind! Hail! Your dog may hide in the bathroom when these happen, but we'll be there for you. Floods, though, aren't covered.

Liberty tries to copy Lemonade Product

Daniel and Insurance Great Hank Greenberg

Ty at his "Retirement" Party (July 2017)

Finding a Reinsurer

Before we could operate as an insurance company, we needed something called reinsurance. Obtaining that would be the next phase in our journey. Largely unknown outside the insurance space, this somewhat mysterious product simply is insurance that insurance companies buy to protect themselves against paying out of their own pocket all the losses from the many claims on the insurance policies they sell. It is the insurance company's way to hedge their bets.

Here's how it works: Without reinsurance, many insurance companies are just a few natural disasters away from real trouble. To avoid large loss events (called catastrophic or CAT events) from forcing insurance companies into state receivership (i.e., the insurance version of bankruptcy), insurance companies sell some of their risk to other insurers. They have to pay the reinsurers part of the premium the insurance company collects from its insured; in turn, the reinsurer will pay some of the losses.

Reinsurance is a critical part of financial stability for an insurance company—and suffice to say regulators would not allow Lemonade to be an insurance company unless it bought sufficient reinsurance from quality reinsurers approved by state regulators. From a reinsurer's point of view, the key to making a profit is spread of risk. Put simply, reinsurers generally are more willing to take the risk of a large portfolio of insureds going bad: The larger the size of the group being reinsured, the safer the bet for the reinsurer.

When I met with Daniel and Shai in May 2015, my Number 1 fear was that we would not be able to buy the right type and amount of reinsurance. Not only were we a startup, but our business model was asking reinsurers to do the very opposite of what they usually insist upon. Instead of asking them to take the risk that the entire portfolio of all Lemonade policies would, as a whole, have large losses, we would be asking them to go along with our idea of creating dozens— indeed, many hundreds—of individual small groups (some with as few as a hundred people) and take the risk that any one (or more) of these groups could have large losses. In other words, we were going to ask our reinsurers to potentially repay some of our losses on any group, regardless of how much money we were making on the other groups. Each group was separate.

This violates a fundamental tenet of a reinsurer's profitability: the law of large numbers. Reinsurers typically will reinsure an insurance company's entire portfolio of policies as a single whole, knowing that a segment of those policies may have unexpected losses but also that it is doubtful (absent a CAT event) that the entire portfolio will have an overall large loss. Reinsurers seek to safeguard their position and profits by reinsuring the performance of only the whole portfolio. Lemonade was asking our reinsurers to forget that rule—which I thought at the beginning to be a difficult if not impossible task.

So, how to do the impossible? Most reinsurance companies want to sell through a reinsurance broker. So our first step was to find one and, given the task above, it had to be a very good one. I started out by considering the firms owned by giants. Marsh & McLennan and Aon, for example, the two largest insurance brokers in the world, both have their own reinsurance broker subsidiary: Guy Carpenter in the case of

Marsh, and Aon Benfield in the case of Aon. You might say that those are the gorillas in the field.

I had dealt with both in the past, and I knew they were both talented. But I wondered what they would think of Lemonade.

Dan Glaser, a former AIG colleague, had recently become CEO of Marsh & McLennan, so I called Glaser and asked to meet him for breakfast. He agreed, and soon we were buttering toast on good china together in his offices at 1166 Avenue of the Americas in New York City. I was aware that Dan might not be such a fan of my new venture. Lemonade's business model was to sell insurance directly to the consumer, not through an insurance broker, and Dan was CEO of the largest insurance broker in the world. Lemonade's model, at least in theory, was a direct threat to him.

Despite this, I knew that Dan would not throw me out of his office for at least two reasons. First, the higher you go up the insurance ladder, the more you find people who think expansively. They see the world through bigger lenses. Second, I knew Dan. We had spent a lot of time together back at AIG, and if anyone in the insurance brokerage leadership could understand the revolution Lemonade represented and would want to be close to it, it was Dan Glazer. So, I laid out my need for a top reinsurance broker to Dan. His response was immediate: "Ty," he said, "we would like to help you."

Dan sent me to John Trace, a US President of Guy Carpenter, the reinsurance brokerage subsidiary of Marsh & McLennan. John put together a top team led by David Duffy, one of the most creative and nicest people I know in reinsurance. Dave immediately became part of the Lemonade family, and, like me, he soon put together a great list of possible reinsurers who might be able to think out of the box.

First on both our lists was XL Catlin, led by Michael McGavick. A former candidate for Congress, Mike is truly one of the great innovative thinkers in insurance. I had known Mike for several years. Not too long before I began working with Lemonade, Mike and I had put together an innovative product to insure the theft of bitcoins. I knew XL could be our lead reinsurer, but I needed to get to Mike directly, and he is a busy guy. (A couple of years later, Mike would sell XL Catlin to the large French insurer AXA for $15.3 billion.)

Fortunately, Mike was scheduled to give a speech at New York's John Street Club, an association for insurance executives. I was a member. His speech, unsurprisingly, was about innovation. He told the audience of traditional insurers that "[w]e must all start to think like unicorns [a term describing a privately held startup valued at $1 billion] if we are to survive," adding that "[i]f we as an insurance industry do not become more innovative, we will become *irrelevant*."

What a statement! I thought. As any psychologist will tell you, one of the worst feelings a person can have is to believe that he or she has become *irrelevant*. Mike was telling a group of the most senior insurance executives in the nation that their innermost worst fear—the fear of irrelevance—would happen if they did not start doing things differently.

After the speech, I went up to Mike and told him that I was involved in a new company with a funny name, which I thought he would find interesting. He was gracious enough to immediately say "Ty, let's meet."

Soon Daniel Schreiber, Dave Duffy, and I were headed up to Connecticut to meet with Mike McGavick and his second-in-command Greg Hendrick. Daniel gave his usual brilliant presentation, including our initial thoughts on how we thought reinsurance might work given Lemonade's unique model, but again with no numbers, no charts, and no estimates of revenue or profits. Mike lived up to his reputation to spot true innovation. He then turned to Greg and asked what he thought of the reinsurance arrangement we briefly outlined. Greg thought for a moment and then silently moved over the white board in the room and started drawing diagrams, arrows, and numbers. After fifteen minutes of straight work, we all looked at Greg's masterpiece. In fifteen minutes, at the first meeting, Greg drew a new method of reinsurance.

At the end of the meeting, Mike looked at Daniel and me and said, "XL wants to be your reinsurer. I'll make money, I think. As importantly, we want to be an investor." XL became our lead reinsurer, and, though XL Innovate, led our Series A investment round a couple of months later, winning us another $13 million in investment funding on top of the original $13 million seed round. With XL on board as our lead reinsurer, we had quickly caught the attention of other major reinsurance companies, including Hiscox, a large Lloyd's of London syndicate, and even Warren Buffett's Berkshire Hathaway organization. Everyone seemed to want in.

By December 2015, we were still months away from our first license and the right to sell even a single insurance policy. But we had $26 million in the bank, top-flight reinsurers—and new doors kept opening.

Finding a Rating Agency

Any company that wishes to sell insurance in the United States has to be rated for financial stability by a third-party rating agency. This will be required by every state regulator in every state in which you want to do business, so don't even think about filing for an insurer's license if you aren't certain that you will possess a good financial rating. The big gorilla for rating insurance companies is A.M. Best in New Jersey—but if you are a startup, it is next to impossible to get a rating from them, much less a good one. So we didn't even try. Instead, we targeted a fellow disruptor in the insurance field: Demotech.

Demotech was created in 1985 when the insurance industry was battling with how to survive the severe hurricanes hitting the southeast of the United States. The solution found by most of the traditional insurers at the time? Get out of Dodge, i.e. traditional insurers exited the loss-prone areas of the country. This, in turn, led to the creation of *new* insurance carriers to fill in the gap. But, as was still to be the case thirty years later in 2015, these new 1985 insurance carriers had problems getting a financial rating. Demotech was created to solve the problem. Launched in Columbus, Ohio, where the state motto is "With God, all things are possible," Demotech tackled an area of the country where other rating agencies feared to tread: hurricane-prone Florida. Led by Joseph Petrelli, Demotech has been a can-do company from the start, willing to look at startup insurance companies in ways that A.M. Best couldn't.

The problem was that, despite all my contacts in the insurance industry, I didn't know a soul there.

Could I just cold call them? What was I going to say? Would they give the time of day to an insurance startup founded by two technologists from a foreign country? Having nothing to lose, I gave it a go. To my delight, they were receptive. We found them to be excellent people to deal with, and we felt fortunate that they were interested in doing business with us.

Honesty is the best policy. We opened our books so Demotech could evaluate our financial condition. The leaders at Demotech are skilled financial and operational analysts and certainly knew what they were doing. Besides, it was a good dress rehearsal for what the insurance regulators would be doing before deciding whether to give us a license to operate.

Rating agencies are tough, and Demotech is no exception. Insurance companies that hope to earn a rating from them must adhere to a number of requirements. Most of the requirements were financial in nature, and no one was tougher than Demotech. Other requirements were operational—e.g., investigating our means of making sure our customers were satisfied. They looked at everything, even a requirement that every insurance company being rated have a fax machine and a telephone landline so that customers have a means to contact them. A landline kind of made sense, but a fax machine? In 2016? When I told our cofounder Shai Wininger about the fax machine requirement, he looked at me like "What's a fax machine?" Being from a high-tech culture, our founders Daniel and Shai knew that no respectable Millennial (our target customer) would be caught dead using a fax machine. But a requirement is a requirement, so it was my job to make it happen as soon as possible—which meant within twenty-four hours because we were going to have an in-person inspection of our office, the last step in the rating analysis process, the next day.

Mind you, we were in a very hip, highly connected WeWork office, and some of the younger folks among us had never even heard of a fax or used a landline. But the management there helped us out. They advised me to get a VOIP (voice over internet protocol) office phone. The WeWork managers said it would take two weeks to get one. I asked, "How about one day?" "No can do," came their reply. I went on Amazon and had one delivered the next day via Amazon Prime.

The phone arrived, but I had no idea how to install it. It looked nice on an official-looking company desk, but there was no dial tone. I tried everything I could with no success. It was literally fifteen minutes before Demotech arrived by the time I finally figured out how to get a dial tone.

In the end, Demotech didn't even pick up our useless office landline phone to check if we had a dial tone. Maybe they knew what we were actually using was a VOIP toll-free number automatically routed to the department member's cell phone in charge of whatever issue the caller was calling about. At any rate, we got our "A" rating.

With reinsurance and an "A" insurance financial rating in hand, we were finally ready to file for our license.

Getting Our First License

November 2015. It had only been 90 days since Maya and I opened the office in the WeWork Financial District, but Lemonade was on a roll. We were bringing on great people. We had secured funding. We had found top-flight reinsurers, and we secured (subject to getting our insurance carrier license) an "A" financial rating. Now we were ready to file for our first state license, which would allow us to operate as an insurance carrier. If we didn't succeed, all our past achievements would be meaningless. Unless we could convince a state insurance regulator to give this small, startup company founded by two technology executives a license to write insurance, we would have to fold up shop and go home.

Eventually, of course, we would need multiple state licenses—one for every state in which we planned to serve. That's right: Unlike almost every other country in the world, the United States has no national system for insurance regulation; this is done by our fifty states, one state at a time (plus the District of Columbia, Puerto Rico, etc.)

So where to start? Which state should be first? It is an important decision for every insurer because your first state, called your domestic regulator, has more power over your company than any other state regulator. Making the wrong choice about your domestic regulator will have severe consequences when it comes time to seek licenses from other states.

We knew we wanted to have a state with a reputation of being a "tough regulator," one known to be not easy to please if you are the entity being regulated as the one to give us our first license and have the most power over us. Why? The logic is simple. If one of the regulators from whom a new insurance carrier would have the most difficulty convincing to give it a license DOES give you a license, other states will most easily follow. While there are a number of states with a reputation of "toughness," for us, our choice boiled down to California or New York. Both have reputations of being tough—really tough—insurance regulators. Because the team lives in New York, we decided on New York, hoping that Old Blue Eyes was right. The name of the New York department in charge of both banking and insurance is called New York Department of Financial Services, or NYDFS. We expected that convincing NYDFS to give us an insurance license would not be easy. Heavy hangs the head that wears the title of insurance commissioner, the head insurance state regulator, since he or she is charged with making sure that tens of millions of dollars of insurance claims are paid. The amount of loss a carrier can be at risk for in any given policy can be 1,000 times the amount of premium received for that risk. Because of this, insurance regulators have multiple financial and operational requirements, including capital requirements, minimum surplus balance, and minimum cash on hand to do business. Insurance regulators have discretion as to how many and what requirements to insist upon before giving an insurance company a license to operate. The newer the company, the more might be required. So, given Lemonade's startup nature, we expected that New York would add a few more requirements than usual before they would issue us a license, assuming we could convince them to give us a license at all.

New York does not grant licenses lightly. We had to win approval from NYDFS's entire team of insurance actuaries, lawyers, and regulators assigned to our case. But we knew Lemonade had a good case to make: firm financials, great reinsurers, and an acceptable financial rating. We also knew that our insurance operations were managed by seasoned insurance professionals with hundreds of years of combined experience at some of the top global insurance companies. In other words, we had a good story. But would it be good enough for New York?

Our first decision pertained to how we should approach the regulators. Do we mention right away our unique business model to give "excess" profits to charity rather than keeping it ourselves or try to portray ourselves, at least initially, as "just another insurance company" seeking to do business in New York and let them know about the differences later on? In theory, the more we sounded just like every other insurance company, the easier it might be to get a license, but could we start a new business with a planned foundation of transparency with anything less than the full transparency right from the start? In the end, this was another easy decision: We started the meeting with New York with how we were different from any other insurance company who probably asked them for a license. We would not shy away from the uniqueness of the Lemonade concept, warts and all.

It was then that we realized that things that had seemed simple to us appeared complex to regulators. For example, we explained our charitable contribution plan to regulators as plainly as possible: Lemonade would take a fixed 20 percent of all premiums. The rest would go to pay claims and pay for reinsurance. If there were money left over, it would go to the charities chosen by the policyholders. "Simple," we said. "Not so simple," they replied. Was this an illegal rebate, they asked? Was it an illegal dividend, they inquired? This has never been done (read approved) before, they said.

All insurance companies are required to maintain a certain premium-to-surplus ratio, which is exactly what it sounds like: For X amount in premium, the company must have Y amount in minimum cash/securities in the bank. The common ratio is 3:1, meaning that if Lemonade wrote $300 million in premium, it would to maintain a capital account of at least $100 million. It sounds straightforward enough, but it was of great concern to New York licensures.

Ever since Superstorm Sandy hit in 2012 and caused massive insurance losses, New York has been increasingly concerned about small insurance companies having enough funds on hand to withstand such an event. Could our new little company pass their test? Would we be asked to maintain more capital than the regulatory standard "premium to surplus" ratio of 3:1?

If we were to be asked to commit more capital in order to comply with something higher than the standard 3:1 ratio, we would be forced to dip further in to our VC funds, largely because the capital of an insurance company basically just sits in conservative bank accounts earning virtually no interest (at least in 2015). Using VC funds in this way would mean those funds weren't working to help the company grow, something VCs insist upon.

Minimum capital was only one of several issues on which we had to come to an agreement with the NYDFS. After a few months of pleasant but ultimately unproductive (at least to me) meetings, we knew that we needed help to move things along. To be fair, New York was moving as fast as possible, especially given the task of approving a new type of insurance company like ours. The NYDFS team was smart and capable. But we still were hoping that things *might* move a bit faster if we could just get the personal attention of the Superintendent of NYDFS, the head regulator for the entire banking and insurance industries in New York State. The question was how. Trying to get her attention in the wrong way could easily backfire, and we didn't want to disrespect the people in NYDFS who were already working on the Lemonade license application.

As luck would have it, at the time we were trying to figure out how to get DFS to move things along a bit faster without annoying the hell of them, Daniel was introduced to Bradley Tusk. Bradley had developed a reputation for taking on difficult assignments and getting people to the table that no one else could. It was just a short time earlier that Bradley had convinced New York Mayor Bill de Blasio to come to the negotiation table with the ride-share company Uber, who was having problems operating in New York City due to the opposition by the city's powerful Taxi & Limousine Commission. Bradley was intrigued by Lemonade and thought he might be able to help us get the right level of attention in the New York Department of Financial Services. We were interested but concerned. Would Bradley, who had earned his stripes using high-intensity tactics against the mayor's office on behalf of Uber, be able to play a gentler game against the NYDFS? After all, unlike Uber, Lemonade would forever be heavily regulated by the New York insurance department and would need to maintain a solid relationship with them. Getting attention is one thing; causing hostile feelings in your most important regulator is another.

As it turned out, Bradley and his team outdid themselves. With their help, we soon got the personal attention of New York's superintendent of financial services, Maria Vullo. She had just gotten the position a few months earlier, in June 2016, so there were a lot more important things on her mind than Lemonade, but we managed to get her attention anyway. She asked Scott Fischer, the executive deputy superintendent—essentially the New York commissioner of insurance—who reported to her, to take personal charge.

Scott soon came down to Manhattan from Albany to check out the situation. His mandate: make a decision about Lemonade one way or the other. Scott Fisher is one of the most talented insurance regulators I know. Smart, practical, and insightful, and a lawyer to boot, he is no pushover. We knew we had our job cut out for us in order to convince him to give us our license, but we also soon discovered that Scott's combination of intelligence, legal talent, and practicality made him the perfect partner for our negotiations. He wanted to know more about the giveback—how exactly did it work? His questions were good, as were questions from Stephen Doody, deputy superintendent for property and casualty insurance at NYDFS and the person who ultimately would greenlight Lemonade for its license. Both men emphasized the department's need to protect New York consumers.

Still the process dragged on. Negotiation after negotiation, month after month—and yet no license. Meanwhile, we were anxious to start operations. I have long ago realized that in business as in much of life, setting a deadline is critical. Announcing a new business in New York after October is never wise unless it is a Christmas business, so when we thought we were close to a final agreement with Scott, Stephen, and their team, we picked a date: September 21, 2016, almost exactly one year from the date Maya and I opened the New York office. There is also another old rule in business and in life. Forge ahead and *sometimes* burn the bridge behind you so you can't go back. With this philosophy firmly in mind, we prepared our operations. The press was notified of the launch date, holding our press release in embargo until 7 a.m. on September 21, 2016. By announcing the date to the press, we burned the bridge behind us. We had to get our license by then or face the PR nightmare of not delivering on our first promise. As a practical matter, the real deadline was a week before launch date, September 14, 2016. That was the very last day we could tell the press that the launch date was being postponed.

DFS's review of our application was completed. We were just waiting for their answer. There were no guarantees that we would get the license, and of course, no guarantee that we would get it by September 14. In the late afternoon of September 13, 2016, Bill Latza and I were in his office waiting for the email approving our license. We were pretty sure we had successfully answered all of DFS's questions, but we also knew that anything could happen. More questions or requests for additional information can always be made. If 5 p.m. rolled around and we didn't have the license, I would have to make a very painful call to Daniel. If we didn't get the approval we needed before the press release hit the streets, it would be a media disaster.

The minutes ticked by. At 4:50 p.m. the email finally landed in my inbox: "Enclosed please find …" We had made it, and with a full ten minutes to spare! I couldn't wait to call Daniel.

It had taken us ten months from first conversation with DFS to obtaining a license to operate an insurance company in New York. I am told that it is the shortest application period of any new insurance company in the history of New York State.

The Launch

The day had finally come. Barely seventeen months since I first spoke to Daniel, that ordinary day in an April 2015 was now ancient history. After months of sustained effort, we had received our license to sell insurance in New York. Now we could launch.

The big day was here: September 21, 2016. We had finally put in place an insurance policy that could be purchased from a smartphone or other mobile device in less than three minutes—and for as little as $5 a month.[4] Would there be any takers? As Daniel was apt to say in those days, "Would the dog eat the dog food?"

Of course, our target market, Millennials, is one of the most precocious generations ever raised (I know because I helped to raise some of them). Intuit CEO Brad D. Smith has said of this generation that it is "shaping technology." He explains: "This generation has grown up with computing in the palm of their hands. They are more socially and globally connected through mobile internet devices than any prior generation. And they don't question; they just learn." Could we reach

---

4   Without brokers or agents, and without issuing policies in paper, we were able to drive prices for a simple renter's policy down to $5 per month, less than half of what the competition was charging.

this group?

We were all waiting to learn the answer to that question. The small Lemonade team at Tel Aviv was flown to New York and joined the New York team along with Daniel and Shai, all staring at the same screen—a large monitor on the wall which would instantly show any purchase of a Lemonade insurance policy. At 7 a.m. EDT, we had flipped the switch, as it were, making Lemonade insurance policies available to any New Yorker. And, so, there we were, standing around waiting for the first sale to be recorded. We had set it up that with each sale a ring would sound. It was as exciting and tension-filled as watching the moon landing; this launch was our moon landing, and our first policy-holder would be our Neil Armstrong.

Honestly, I was a bit scared. For the first few minutes after we went live, there was dead silence—except for the loud thoughts in my head:

What were we thinking? No brokers, no agencies, no advertising, not a single subway poster, not a single billboard, no radio ads, no late-night TV pitchmen, no funny ads with sound effects on the radio, no billboard on the New Jersey turnpike. Just a lot of chatter on social media. I was crazy to think this would work.

It took only six minutes before our own Neil landed. We heard the sound we were waiting for: BING! At 7:31 a.m., our first renter's policy popped into the system. We had our first $5 in revenue. Seconds later, more signs of life: BING! BING! BING! By the end of the day, we had more than 70 policies sold! Later we would announce the results of the first 48 hours of being in business: 36,110 people visiting our home page from 163 countries, including 4,570 New Yorkers, almost 2000 people downloaded the Lemonade App from the Apple Store or Google Play, an incredible 14.8% conversion rate from seeing our price to buying the insurance.

Our team of internal search engine optimizers and social network experts in Tel Aviv had successfully created awareness of the Lemonade product—without a spending a single penny on traditional advertising—and we were in business.

It was amazing. Why did these buyers trust a new insurance company with a funny name? We had no logo of hands holding, no rock in middle of ocean. We had no famous brand or age-old reputation to trade on. Yet that first day we welcomed seventy new customers. Two years later, we would be selling a new policy *every 60 seconds, 24 hours a day, seven days a week*, but, for me, the sweetest was that first day's seventy.

The eventual flood of early new policies did not come without cost in time and attention—and with a few mistakes. For example, we originally thought that our target market, Millennials, would be completely glued to their screens and eager to use our user interfaces. We didn't think they needed, or wanted, to talk to a real person; just in case, though, we provided on the Lemonade website the office telephone number—that old Demotech landline we thought would be just for show. As it turned out, while the vast majority of our customers preferred to email their customer service questions, those copper wires were still burning as many phone calls came in from our so-called high-tech generation. It turns out a portion of our target customers still wanted to deal with a human. So much for the texting-only generation.

This turned one of our core values on end. Being both all-internet and all-automated was a core value to our founders, especially to Shai, and it turned out to be wrong (or, at least, not totally right). Sometimes, people—even Millennials—want to talk to people. Not always, but often enough.

As a consultant in insurance innovation, I often see founders who cling to every core value despite the facts. They usually are not successful. Not with Shai. Without hesitating a moment, Shai saw the data highlighting the number of callers we were fielding and admitted he had made a mistake. I had admired Shai since the day we first met, but this made me see him in an even greater light. A founder who could reverse course on a core belief is a rare individual indeed.

So, with this surprising data in hand, we decided to build a customer service presence—not through outsourcing (we would have no call center in India or otherwise) but a true customer service team right in our New York office. They would be full-time employees of Lemonade, not independent contractors jumping from one company to another. Customer service employees soon accounted for a third of our New York organization as we grew from a staff of twelve to eighteen. In a true sense of the word, these folks were (and are) the real Lemonade Makers, talking to our customers and solving their problems.

Of course, our new customers reached us not only via the phone lines. The internet still led many customers to us. Indeed, soon enough, Twitter and Facebook were filling up with praise from customers. Most of our reviews are 5 or 4 stars, although, of course, over time we have had our share of complaints, typically because we couldn't provide a coverage feature that some of our competitors could. These complaints allowed us to learn and grow. In light of such feedback, we often went back to the drawing board, added the feature or created a better one, and made it available.

Later, my successor, John Peters, would write: "We have the good fortune of having a strong, rapidly growing base of customers who trust us, and whom we trust, too. Together, we are building a company for the long haul, and the early metrics make me feel like we are on the right path."

Everything was off to a great start. Which is when you really need to worry.

Who Are Those Guys?

O ne of my favorite movie quotes is from *Butch Cassidy and the Sundance Kid*. A mysterious posse is chasing the heroes, played respectively by Paul Newman and Robert Redford, and the two bank robbers keep turning around and asking, "Who are those guys?"

During our first few months of selling insurance, I often thought of those scenes when looking out for our competitors, the industry's heavyweight homeowner's and renter's insurance carriers, not because they were paying attention to us, but because they weren't. Our competitors didn't even notice us coming for the longest time. By the time they did, it was too late: We had overtaken them in our target market—tech-savvy Millennials, especially in the urban apartment rental space. We had obtained 1 percent of the New York renter's insurance market in less than nine months, which was an unheard-of achievement in the heavily competitive New York insurance market.[5]

The slow response from our competitors puzzled me, at least at first. When we started Lemonade, we got a lot of favorable publicity from the media and from our customers. We naturally expected to see

---

5   By the end of our second year, our marketshare has grown 6 fold to 6% of the New York renters insurance market and #1 in new business acquisition.

the best insurance companies in the world to go after us. But nobody was in sight. This was heartening and frightening at the same time.

The heartening part was that this meant that we were truly disruptive. Experts such as Clayton Christensen of Harvard University often remark that true disrupters are not noticed by the industry they are disrupting until it is too late. The reason for this is that disrupters usually start in a very narrow space, essentially scratching at your competitor's small toe. The usual reaction of the competitor is "I don't care about my toe" and ignores the disruptor. But then the disrupter moves up to the ankle. And the competitor will say, "Well, it's only my ankle. I'm not really worried." This continues until disruptors are at the throat of their competitors, and by then it is too late for the competition to do anything to stop the advance.

Such seemed to be the case with Lemonade. Months and months went by when we were taking an increasingly larger percentage of the New York renters' market, and yet no one noticed. Then we expanded to Illinois and California, and again, it seemed we had magical powers of invisibility. The big insurers seemed to have no idea that we existed. When we expanded to Texas, we felt sure that we would be noticed. But no.

Meanwhile, a 2016 survey conducted by PWC showed that 74 percent of insurance executives believed that their industry would be substantially disrupted by FinTech technology.[6] The same survey indicated that most insurance companies were doing nothing or next to nothing about this belief. At least, for the moment. And that was the frightening part for we knew it couldn't last and had no idea what would happen when our "honeymoon" from competition ended.

Eventually, of course, we started seeing some evidence that the competition did know who we were. But their reaction, seemed, well,

---

6   Dariush Yazdani, Gregory Weber, et al. "Blurred Lines: How FinTech Is Shaping Financial Services," Global FinTech Report. March 2016. London: PWC Global. Retrieved June 13, 2018, from https://www.pwc.ru/en/banking/publications/fintech-global- report-eng.pdf

a bit bizarre. One of the largest homeowner's insurance carriers (not to be named) created an insurance product geared toward Millennials; their advertisements for that product featured a yellow drink, and their website was almost a direct copy of Lemonade's. Here is a key to innovation strategy: If you want to show your customers that you are innovative, don't copy the innovations developed by others.

I also remember that, by pure accident in the week that Lemonade went live, GEICO happened to put on a cute commercial featuring the rapper Ice-T at a lemonade stand.[7] As I recall, the commercial ended with Ice-T looking into the camera saying, "What's with these people, man. Lemonade. Read the sign. Lemonade." And, just think, GEICO didn't ask us to pay a penny for repeating our name over and over.

At the time of writing of this book, yet another traditional insurer is offering a renter's policy geared toward Millennials. They, too, tried to copy the look and feel of Lemonade, but as is the case with almost all legacy companies, their tech and infrastructure simply cannot be sufficiently modified to be true cutting edge. They turned out to be a poor copycat.

The lesson is that disruptive innovation is almost impossible for long-established legacy companies. (see sidebar) To survive, whether in the insurance industry or any other industry, such companies must either partner with disruptive startups, buy an existing successful one (and, if they are wise, continue to allow it to run separately from the "mother ship" that bought it) or create a completely separate subsidiary also not tied to the "mother ship." Outside the insurance industry, Nestlé Group is successfully using this technique with their Nespresso product subsidiary. Within the insurance industry, many insurance carriers today are pursuing with some success the partnership route, including XL Catlin (soon to be a part of AXA, the large French insurer) and Munich Re in Germany, to name a couple.

---

7   Alexandra Jardine. "Ice T Runs a Lemonade Stand in This Funny Geico Spot," AdAge. September 9, 2016. Retrieved June 13, 2018, from http://creativity-online.com/work/geico-lemonade-not-ice-t/48972

Lessons in Innovation from Startups

Up until 4 years ago, my entire career has been in innovation at large legacy insurance companies, managing teams that invented such products as Y2k Insurance, cyber insurance and corporate reputation insurance. I was at the top of the game. AIG had the reputation of the being the most innovative insurance company around (for better or for worse) and I headed up innovation at the company *globally*.

In a short few months I learned that Wall Street has nothing on Silicon Valley when it comes to true innovation. It isn't just because legacy companies have intrenched IT systems that are difficult and expensive to change. It isn't just because legacy companies are composed of senior managers running multi-million-dollar divisions and are just too busy in their day to day survival building a business to think, no less actually do something, about creating a business.

The reason why legacy companies can only accomplish incremental innovation and not disruptive innovation is because the mentality of a startup is fundamentally different than a legacy company.

Two specific case examples I learned from my days at Lemonade illustrate the point.

When I headed up innovation divisions in legacy companies and created new products, our mentality was to try to launch the perfect product, one that we would never have to change. Early on after I joined Lemonade, Shai said to me "we trying to create MVP here." For the life of me I couldn't figure out how "Most Valuable Player" had anything to do with what we were trying to accomplish. Moshe whispered in my ear "Ty, MVP stands for "Minimally Viable Product." A "minimally viable product" is one that just barely works. It meets the <u>minimum</u> goals for the product and is expected and intended to be frequently and rapidly improved. I thought these guys were crazy. "Are you saying", I said to Moshe, "that we are *planning* to be imperfect?"

The other major disconnect was when I first heard about "A/B Testing." A/B Testing is the concept that you rapidly send into the marketplace multiple different versions of something and see what works. Again, this is the direct opposite of how legacy companies work. When Shai first mentioned this to me, I said "you mean you try 'B' when 'A' doesn't work?". He said "No Ty. We try 'B' regardless even if 'A' seems to be working well." I walked away simply shaking my head. Why try something else when the thing you are using works just fine.

It wasn't simply that I hadn't heard of the phrase "MVP" or "A/B Testing", it was the very *concept* was foreign to me.

Well, it was not very long before I realized that everything I learned in innovation was wrong. You see what MVP and A/B Testing has in common is that it is the natural result of understanding that it is your customers, and no one else, that determines whether your product is a success, and that it is the height of arrogance to think otherwise.

Don't have a goal to launch a perfect product. Don't try to figure out the "right" answer. Instead, understand that whatever you may think is the "right solution", it is your customer's view that is the only one that counts. Thus, get the product out as quickly as you can so your customers can tell you what's wrong with it. Try rapid different approaches so your customer can tell you which one they prefer.

That's true "customer centric" innovation. A concept foreign (excepet as a marketiing phrase) to legacy companies if they were to be really truthful with themselves, but part of the very DNA of a startup.

For the startup disruptive innovator, there is analogous trap: planning your exit strategy. An exit strategy tries to figure out what you will do with the company if you are successful: IPO? Acquisition? If you ask us at Lemonade what our exit plan was, we would answer that we've had none. And that, in my mind, is the only right answer. If you are going to be successful, don't worry about an exit plan. Instead, create a product that is valued by your customers. Exit will take care of itself.

Sea to Shining Sea

Even before our competitors started noticing us, we knew that in order to survive, we needed to keep on growing. From Day 1, we could not be just a New York insurance carrier specializing in renter's insurance. With Daniel having spent a substantial amount of his life in California's Silicon Valley—and with all due respect to New York's Silicon Alley—we had to Go West. So, it was California, here we come.

Truth be told, we already had begun conversations with John Finston, general counsel and deputy insurance commissioner for the State of California before we even finalized New York. Californians and New Yorkers argue about who is the toughest insurance regulator, but I have to say that it's a draw. What this meant for Lemonade was that while establishing an insurance company in New York might make it easier for us to get licenses in other states, it wouldn't necessarily help getting one in fiercely independent California.

I have found California insurance regulators to be some of the smartest and most creative people I have ever met. John Finston was an excellent example. A top-flight lawyer and no-nonsense regulator, John also was part of the Silicon Valley culture, recognizing and supporting smart innovation wherever he found it. Because of that, and although

I knew that it might take months to get a license, I was hopeful that the Lemonade model would find a place in the state that is regarded by many people as the home of technology.

Over the course of months, we met several times with California insurance regulators. John Finston led the team assigned to us. Bill Latza played the key role, just as he did in New York. With the two of them handling some key issues, it felt like we were in good hands. And, of course, that's when a problem appears.

Toward the end of our negotiations, when we had almost everything figured out, John told us that he was retiring from public service and would later join the large national law firm, Drinker Biddle. I panicked. Without John at the helm until the very end, I feared that we would never get our license. Fortunately, I was wrong. The rest of John's team carried on without pause, and just six months after we got our New York license, we won our license in California.

That day was a big deal for us. Silicon Valley was in the heart of California, and it was every technology company's dream to do business there. So we all did the logical thing: We went to a neighborhood bar and insisted that they play only California songs. All night we sang, from the Beach Boys' "California Girls" to the Eagles' "Hotel California." We were drinking beer and spreading "Good Vibrations" all around.

Alas, morning always comes, and there were more states in which we wanted to get licenses and more work to be done. With the East Coast and West Coast anchored, it was time to go to the middle of America, and that meant Illinois.

Every region has its own risks, so once again we had to change our mindset—and our underwriting formulas. New York has floods; California has earthquakes, mudslides, and brush fires; the Midwest has tornadoes. Could our little company conduct an analysis of risk to be so versatile? Absolutely yes.

Going for our license in Illinois was important, but it was an effort

I would lean out of. By now I had taken off one of my hats—chief underwriting officer—and given it to John Peters, who had come over to Lemonade from Liberty Mutual. John had all the wisdom of traditional insurance values. With John's help, our negotiations in Illinois quickly met with success.

In January 2017, our next biggest challenge came: Texas. Everything is big in Texas, including insurance risks. In Texas, the big peril was hail. In April of the previous year, for example, a single hailstorm produced more than $1.4 billion in insurance losses, one of the state's most costly. It was tough to convince the traditional regulators in Texas to allow a small startup to insure their homes and apartments. Could Lemonade handle losses if another hailstorm like that happened? The Texas regulators scrutinized our reinsurance contracts, surplus capital position, and financial statements and applied various probable maximum loss scenario tests before eventually concluding that Lemonade was strong enough to handle Texas.

So now we were operating in four of the largest states in the country: California, Illinois, New York, and Texas. Licenses for other states started coming even more quickly. Once we had won licenses in about a dozen of the most influential states, including New Jersey and Connecticut (the home of a number of major insurance companies), others, even those which were initially reluctant about this new type of insurance company, came around. Approvals started pouring in.

According to sociologists, a tipping point is that moment in time when a large number of group members changes behavior by adopting a previously rote practice. In innovation theory, this occurs only once the new product or design is an actual improvement over the previous design and when the cost of moving away from the existing product is low enough to encourage openness to the change. In other words, you get to a point in your company or product maturity when it is more difficult *not* to gain acceptance and speed. Finally, that was us!

That's not to say that everything in our state licensing strategy went easily for us. Florida, for example, was a challenge. Florida is important to any carrier thinking about homeowner's insurance because it holds more than 10 percent homeowner's market and because it is a huge state for personal lines insurers. However, with its risk of severe hurricanes, it also is one of the most loss-prone states in which to operate. Definitely not for the faint of heart. However, our plan was to provide insurance for renters only, which, in theory, was much less risky.

We had good contacts at the Florida Office of Insurance Regulation. They wanted us there, and we wanted to be there. As I said, it's a great state for renters. The problem was that a law in Florida required insurance companies to maintain a high level of capital funds, more than twice that of any other state and more than what we wanted to make available. And it was not just a regulation which, in theory, could be changed by the Office of Insurance Regulation (who liked us); it's an actual <u>law</u>, meaning that *only the Florida legislature* can change it.

We knew that the law on the books, which was designed to make sure homeowner's insurance carriers could pay large hurricane-related losses, was a good idea generally, but we believed that it shouldn't apply to companies like ours that just wanted to do renter's insurance. Because renters suffer much lower losses than homeowners, mandating an insurance carrier to maintain that high amount of capital just to provide renter's insurance just didn't make sense to us. The problem was that the law wasn't written to make that type of company distinction. In other words, the law was illogical, but it was still the law.

The answer? Straightforward enough: Change the law. The challenge: It usually takes at least one year—and often longer—to change an existing insurance law in Florida. Of course, with Florida being such an important state, we really didn't want to spend a year before being allowed to offer renter's insurance in Florida.

So, we tackled the problem in steps. First, we had to determine whether key influencers were on our side. In this case, that meant confirming that the Florida Office of Insurance Regulation that they were in favor of changing the law. They were. Check! Second, find the best local lobbyist that is known for making legislative changes happen fast. We hired the best insurance lobbying firm we could find to locate an influential legislator who understood the need to change the law and who would work with us to do that. Check! We approached the issue using the same logic as we did with seasoning (see sidebar). We found a legislator who agreed with us that the capital funds rule should be rewritten to include an exception for insurers providing renter's insurance. After all, hurricanes do not directly affect renters the way it does homeowners since it is their landlords are the ones who pay for damage to the building structure. Check!

Next problem: Execution. The Florida legislative session is *only sixty days long*. When we had this idea to change the law, the current legislative session had already stated. No one thought we could get a new law passed in a single legislative session. That never happens, we were told. Simply can't be done, we were told. But due to the great insight of two leading legislators, Senator Jeff Brandes and Representative David Santiago, it was, and in a single legislature session! On June 23, 2017, the so-called "Lemonade Amendment" was signed into law by Governor Rick Scott of Florida.

Seasoning

Once you get your first license to operate an insurance company in a particular state (which is called getting your domestic license), you naturally want to get more states if you want to grow your company. However, there is a rule on getting additional state insurance company licenses, called seasoning.

This rule is important and almost universal. Under normal circumstances, a new company with a single license cannot get an additional license outside its initial territory (in our case, New York) until it has been operating for three years. The theory is that a company should be properly "seasoned" before it can be allowed to venture elsewhere. Of course, Lemonade did not want to wait three years before venturing beyond New York. So we did what truly innovative people always do: We looked for the exception to the rule.

It turned out that a new insurance company can get around the seasoning rule if it is offering a "new product to an 'underserved' market." For example, an insurance company may decide to offer a special new plan to insure against losses from earthquakes or other high-severity disasters. Because only a limited number of carriers provide this product, the market is considered "underserved," thus allowing unseasoned insurance carriers to enter.

Problem: In our case, our market was not, on the face of it, "underserved." There were plenty of renter's and homeowner's policies and carriers out there.

Solution: If you don't like the answer, change the question. Put another way, there is an old saying, "Ask the wrong question and you will get the wrong answer."

In our case, I believed that asking whether existing insurance companies were willing to *sell* renter's and homeowner's insurance was the wrong question. Rather, I believed that asking whether Millennials were willing to *buy* renter's insurance from traditional companies was the right question. The answer to the right question was, conveniently for us, a resounding "No." In other words, I argued that Millennials seldom bought renter's insurance, and therefore were, in fact, "underserved" despite the numerous traditional rental policies and rental carriers out there that were more than willing to sell insurance to them.

When I first raised this approach, I couldn't get my colleagues to stop laughing. The lawyers in the room said, "Ty, in the history of insurance regulation, no one has ever interpreted the 'underserved market' exception in the way that you just did. No regulator is going to buy that argument." From a regulator's point of view, underserved is viewed from the point of view of the seller—i.e., are there enough sellers for the product in the market? I was turning that around and asking regulators to look at the issue from the point of view of the buyer. Who cares how many sellers there are, if the buyers don't like any of them?

I had only one thing on my side: logic. If the purpose of the underserved market exception was to make sure that consumers who didn't buy insurance could now buy insurance, Lemonade deserved a license. After all, statistics show that Millennials do not buy renter's insurance, primarily because they don't trust insurance companies and they don't like the process they are forced to use in order to buy insurance. If Lemonade changed all that, and I believed we did, Millennials would now be served for the first time.

It turned out the doubters were wrong. Soon they became full-fledged believers in my "enlightened" interpretation of this decades-old regulatory rule. In the end, we presented the idea of "turning the beat around" with a straight face wherever we went, and we convinced just about each and every regulator of the same.

The lesson is that in legal matters, as in life in general, you don't need to be restrained by the way things have always been. You can get an idea from pure logic and run with it. Believe in yourself—and think for yourself. If your idea is sound, even regulators will listen, eventually.

The Making of Lemonade

Once Lemonade had received licenses in most of the major US states, and now that John Peters was firmly managing the insurance operations, things were starting to move at Lemonade. Jim Hagerman was commanding a larger claims operation, Ron Topping was masterfully handling our financial stability, Yael and Maya continued to be geniuses in their respective areas and Bill Latza was in place as our great general counsel. Now it was time to start thinking about Lemonade's next attempt to make a social impact. And what a topic we chose.

A Dream Tested

Perhaps the most important part of Lemonade is our social impact. For that reason, I've saved this best story for last.

As I explained (in Chapter 4: Who Are We?), Lemonade is a B Corp, which means that we operate with a social aspect. In October 2017, about a year after we started selling insurance in New York, we did something dramatic, something no other insurance company had up to that point done. By that point in time, we already had become the go-to company for renter's (and to a lesser extent, homeowner's) insurance, particularly in urban areas such as New York City. But we don't live in a vacuum. And the incidents of mass shootings in our schools and other places that seemed to be in the news on a regular basis deeply disturbed us. If our decision to become a B Corp were to mean anything, it demanded that we look at the role we play in making society better. Given various shooting incidents around the country (too many and too sickening to name here), we had to confront our role in insuring guns and gun ownership.

At first, we repressed the impulse to do something about it. I can't overstate how very conservative the insurance industry is, has been, and always will be. Insurance companies go with the flow. We are neutral.

We don't want to offend anyone, certainly not potential customers. It has long been unheard-of for an insurance company to even contemplate not insuring a piece of property because of a moral issue. If it is legal to own something, an insurance company will insure it.

Could we limit or refuse to insure guns, just because they are guns? Doing so would be unprecedented.

The topic of common-sense gun control or Second Amendment protection (depending upon your scope of reference) couldn't be more controversial in the United States. And, as with all Americans, the views of our team ranged widely on the subject. One contingent, which did not express a view on gun control either way, strongly argued that insurers simply should not get into the business of embracing social causes or making underwriting decisions based on moral beliefs. We need to serve our customers, they said, and if they own guns that they wish to insure, who were we to judge? This was perhaps the strongest argument in favor of doing nothing. We also heard trepidation from people from hunting families who were concerned about the long-term impact of curtailed insurance. And there was a big debate between Constitutionalists ready to defend the Second Amendment in its broadest interpretation versus ardent gun control advocates who wanted a more common-sense (and, they say, historically accurate) interpretation of the Second Amendment and control all guns. A common view in the middle was that small guns and rifles were okay, but automatic and semiautomatic weapons had no role in civilian life and should be used only by military and police.

At the end of the day, we decided that it would be contrary to who Lemonade was _not_ to take a moral stance. We decided that we would continue to insure rifles and handguns but only up to $2,500. If an insured owned more than $2,500 worth of firearms, we recommended that they go elsewhere. We also decided not to insure assault rifles altogether, stating that it is a core Lemonade belief that civilians have no need for military-grade weapons. Much later, other companies, such as Dick's Sporting Goods and Walmart, would decide to stop selling guns, and insurers, including EMC Insurance, would take antigun ownership positions (although they said this was for financial rather than social reasons). That said, Lemonade was the first to outright refuse to insure some guns.

This position was fine for Millennials on Madison Avenue, but, mind you, these are not all our customers. Many folks in Texas and parts of Illinois were none too pleased. At the end of the day, I think we figured out we lost more money than we gained by taking this stance. But we didn't care. It was the right thing to do.

On a personal note, it seems to me that more today than ever, it is important that people and corporations stand by their beliefs and distance themselves from actions and actors—whatever position they may have or power they may seem to possess—who create chaos and cause destruction whether to one country or to the globe. Lemonade did exactly that. And, speaking for myself, I have never been more proud of any company.

One Year Later—
Lemonade and Beyond

As I write this, it's been about 18 months since I left the day-to-day operations of Lemonade. As I look back, it seems like it had all happened so fast: the meeting with Daniel, the visit to Jerusalem, the first millions, the first employees, the first customers, reinsurance, licensing, launch, and all the subsequent adventures.

Amazingly, it took just three years for Lemonade to evolve from a concept wall of sticky notes in Jerusalem to a leading provider of renter's and homeowner's insurance, licensed in more than twenty-eight states—in which seven out of every ten Americans live—and operating in over twenty, as well as issuing more than a quarter of million insurance policies by this writing, after less than two years in operations.

What's more is that Lemonade is being courted by a number of countries outside the United States and recently announced our intention to expand to Europe. We are caught up in that vector called momentum, moving forward with a rate of speed determined in part by the intrinsic weight of our value proposition and in part by the gravitational pull of the market that gave us our existence.

Today, Lemonade is the darling of InsurTech and of InsurTech venture capitalists. Our initial seed investors, Aleph and Sequoia Capital, led the way for many more. Insurance company venture capital affiliates soon came on board with XL Innovate (the VC arm of XL Catlin) being an early investor, followed by global insurance giant Allianz. In early 2018, our C Round was led by SoftBank out of Tokyo, which joined existing investors General Catalyst, *Google* Ventures (now simply called GV), Sequoia Capital, Thrive Capital, and Tusk Ventures. We even attracted Hollywood money from Ashton Kutcher's Grade A Investments. In our round C financing, we had a pre-money valuation (i.e., the valuation of a company or asset before the additional financing) which has been reported as more than $500 million. Not bad for a sixteen-month-old startup originating from one of the world's smallest nations.

How did it happen? Yes, we worked hard. And, at times we were lucky. Perhaps Thomas Jefferson was right when he said, "I'm a great believer in luck. And I find the harder I work, the luckier I am."

The truth is that Lemonade's rapid growth was the result of a lot of work and brilliant leadership from its two founders, Daniel Scheiber and Shai Wininger, coupled with expertise from some of the most talented and intelligent people I know in all corners of the business. It's all the innovative people behind Lemonade who make it work.

Yet Lemonade's success also is due to its unique business model and philosophy. With its B Corp structure, behavioral economics, and AI, Lemonade is part of a larger trend of innovation in InsurTech.

Although I am retired from the day-to-day operations of Lemonade, I remain on the board of Lemonade Insurance Company and remain close with Daniel, Shai, and everyone else at Lemonade. Although I must confess that with now over 100 people, there are more and more people there I have never met.

Today I am busy with several companies who hope to be the "next Lemonade." But one of the most favorite things I still do, and love doing, is going around the world and talking about Lemonade. The stories you have read in this book are part of my repertoire. To tell these stories, I go wherever insurance companies and clients gather. They advertise "Breakfast With Lemonade" and the crowds seem to come. Only a year ago, if folks had advertised such an event, people would wonder why the event sponsors were advertising what beverage would be served.

I am, and will forever be, grateful to the great people at Lemonade and truly humbled by the experience. As I once said to Daniel, my entire career in innovation led me to Lemonade and the great privilege to have played a small part in creating it.